WALK AROUND

ESSAYS ON POETRY AND PLACE

David Blair

MADHAT PRESS
ASHEVILLE, NORTH CAROLINA

MadHat Press
MadHat Incorporated
PO Box 8364, Asheville, NC 28814

The Library of Congress has assigned
this edition a Control Number of
2019931122

ISBN 978-1-941196-84-7 (paperback)

Cover art and design by Marc Vincenz
Book design by MadHat Press

www.madhat-press.com

First Printing

Table of Contents

for Steve Almond

Where does it take place? Is he writing in Venice? Is he writing about the Venetian war with Greeks? Are you in a garden in 1870 or 1970? Is there a thunderstorm? In 1970, you have something that diverts lightning from striking your house. In 1870, you could not divert it. It struck your house, and your house burned down.

Time and place give you a great deal….

—Stella Adler

There was one kind of berry, a dark red.
I tried it, one by one, and hours apart.
Sub-acid, and not bad, no ill effects;
and so I made home-brew. I'd drink
the awful, fizzy, stinging stuff
that went straight to my head
and play my home-made flute
(I think it had the weirdest scale on earth)
and, dizzy, whoop and dance among the goats.
Home-made, home-made! But aren't we all?
I felt a deep affection for
the smallest of my island industries.
No, not exactly, since the smallest was
a miserable philosophy.

—Elizabeth Bishop, "Crusoe in England"

Remarks on Walking Around Boston

Since I started out wrong-headedly, not sure if there really was a difference between poetry and philosophy, which there sure is, I will say there is a connection between walking, movement, and the actions of consciousness for many philosophers and poets, whose true subject—or better, grounds for subjects—is consciousness. Probably the greatest influence on me as a writer besides my wife Sabrina is that I never drove a car until I was in my mid-thirties, right before our daughter was born. The places I've lived—the Bronx, Boston, North Carolina, and Pittsburgh—I've experienced on my feet. I guess the other thing is I waited tables until I was almost thirty. It gave me a feeling for "the spread." At Fordham, I majored in philosophy, walking, and reading poetry, mostly on my own. They whacked us around with a lot of Aristotle and Aquinas there, so these activities all more or less seemed like various sides of the same experience. The peripatetic everything in the senses.

W. H. Auden writes a form of walking poem that seems somewhat formalized and pedantic in some respects but also jaunty and cosmopolitan. His poems circle back to their beginnings, just as he seems to circle back to his apartment at the end of "A Walk After Dark," which doesn't contain any real imagery at all. His famous ballad, however, which contains plenty of concrete stylized and even borrowed stuff, begins

> As I walked out one evening,
> > Walking down Bristol Street,
> The crowds upon the pavement
> > Were fields of harvest wheat.

Many ballads are accounts of walks, realistic or fabulous. "As I walked out …" "As I went down to Galway town …" "As you came from the holy land / Of Walsingham …" I want to write a ballad. How do I begin this thing? Answer the question "O where have you been, my blue-eyed son?"

There must be several genres of poems that are walks. One genre might be the circular walk which begins and ends like a walk around the block in the same place or even the same line, such as Lorca's "Back from a Walk," the first poem in *Poet in New York*. Another might be the walk that ends at a desired end. And then there are the poems that end in completely unforeseen places. At the end of *Song of Myself*, Whitman tells us to look for him in the dust under our boot-soles. Where is he?

Walks are temporal. They are things in time. This puts them in the world of music, movies, and narrative rather than in the world of static perception. It's natural that, early, satirical and novelistic Eliot imagines a character walking through a city as a way of conceiving time:

> I mount the steps and ring the bell, turning
> Wearily, as one would turn to nod good-bye to Rochefoucald,
> If the street were time and he at the end of the street,
> And I say, "Cousin Harriet, here is the *Boston Evening Transcript*."

Walks have a plot. They begin and end. That they contain so much variety and yet have a form is endlessly surprising, and inspiring.

A friend of mine, Gregory Lawless, describes reading a poem as like watching a parade. I think writing a poem is sometimes like being in a parade and making a movie of the things the parade passes. Only if there was nobody watching the parade, and maybe I was the only person in it. And there is another parade in my head.

The ultimate poet of the largely internal parade is Wallace Stevens. I wonder if it is true that he composed many poems in his head while walking to work at the insurance company and then dictated them to his secretary.

A long time you have been making the trip
From Havre to Hartford, Master Soleil,
Bringing the lights of Norway and all that.

A long time the ocean has come with you,
Shaking the water off, like a poodle,
That splatters incessant thousands of drops,

Each drop a petty tricolor. For this,
The aunts in Pasadena, remembering,
Abhor the plaster of the western horses,

Souvenirs of museums. But, Master, there are
Lights masculine and lights feminine.
What is this purple, this parasol,

This stage-light of the Opera?
It is like a region full of intonings.
It is Hartford seen in a purple light.

I like to think of Stevens walking from his residential neighborhood past the art museum, then seeing the towers of insurance and the white castle spires of the Connecticut State House, just goofing along with his own internal gait. In "The Noble Rider and the Sound of Words," the overall sense of things is that imagination is at play with the things of the world, that there is a lot of back and forth.

As you walk, you become intensely aware in two directions. There is the outer world, and there is your head space. It is not necessary or possible really to keep strict focus on one or the other. They blend together. This seems related to the way we conceive a metaphor or a simile. One thing presents itself to the mind and another thing from somewhere else presents itself as blended in kinship.

As thoughts occur one after another, so do visual impressions. Imagination is not just voice, but an image-making capacity. Thoreau recommends that we *saunter*. For him, the word suggests *sainte terre,* holy land. A walker is a pilgrim, on a journey, a *holy-lander* like the author of *Piers Plowman* or Sir Walter Raleigh with his scallop-shell. And the word *saunter* also suggests an older and more leisurely speed. You can look around and see multiple angles at the same time. A poet of driving and walking, William Carlos Williams says that the only way to see anything is to walk. I doubt he was a very aggressive driver, the way he slows up on the road to the contagious hospital, or maybe he was getting to be one around the time he wrote *Spring and All.*

One of the novelties of walking in the city is that you don't just have to walk. You can also take buses and ride subways and commuter rails, or even ride public boats. City driving in a place like Boston, where there are not many superhighways and the roads are old and cluttered, is nice to me. It is a form of fast walking.

Walking is cardiovascular and bodily and does good things in the brain. Charles Olson, Williams, Ginsberg and Kerouac are among the many mid-century poets who locate the genesis of the poetic line in the breath. If you think of a line as being both psychological and cardiovascular and are not too literal-minded—if you consider that breath is related to heart function—and a line in English is made of stressed and unstressed syllables—it has something like a pulse in it, and there are a number of impressions that arise in a temporal sequence—nouns, images, sensations—then every poem has as its model a walk from one place to another. Pinsky has an improbable and charming description of a poem as a column of air. Perfect, you cannot lean too heavily on it.

Somewhere—*ABC of Reading,* I think—Ezra Pound says that poetry dies when it gets too far from music and music dies when it gets too far away from the dance. We might go to a theater or a practice room and watch a choreographer block out the movements for a number. The dancers are just walking from place to place before anything else happens.

Every poem has as its model a walk from one place to another. That is true of short lyrics, but it is also true of vast works. *The Divine Comedy* is the greatest urban walk adventure ever, as is James Joyce's *Ulysses*. Robert Frost's "Directive" is an urban walk poem set in the woods, an enormous spiritual advance upon "Acquainted with the Night." I say this because Frost is always sharing space with other people, even if they are just imagined figures in his poems. After all, he went to high school up in Lawrence. That was the school in *Welcome Back, Kotter*.

It's possible to write like a walker. It is also possible to read like a walker. When I was an undergraduate, my favorite Jesuit English professor, John Dzeiglewicz, said that he liked *The Waste Land* and *Four Quartets* because he could walk around them and enter them at various places like buildings, churches, I suspected, but he didn't go that far. Eliot's fragmentary poems owe a lot to walking around his cities, Boston, Cambridge and London. They have so much passing information. Eliot is a peripatetic reader as well. He says that "history has many corridors."

There are also a number of poems about walks a poet who is sitting down would like to take. So much for most of them. I tend to trust the order that I think things in, but I do not always get the order right at first. Revising is another walk. What if I walked over there first?

Let's not forget the rhythm of noodling, detours, and the spirit of discovery. Going in and out of used book stores and record shops and places that rent costumes and sell cheap magic sets is good for you. There are fewer of these around lately, but there are still weird shops. Store windows can be pretty good. That's a strange hookah. A few blocks from here, there is a shop that sells rosary beads, Confirmation gifts, and ecclesiastical accoutrement, in case you want to dress up as a bishop. My friend Bruce Kaplan bought a big hat there.

At the end of "Ode to Laziness," Pablo Neruda pours sand from his shoes after poking around at bits of seaweed and stones and seashells at the beach. I can't really talk about that poem much here, as Neruda's peregrinations there also feature a bicycle. So many great

Charles Simic poems feel like finding things and seeing people while walking, and so do all the short poems by Rilke set in Paris, though Rilke only sees a person when that is all he sees.

My Aunt Dale lives in Greenwich Village and naturally walks just about everywhere. She has lived there more than forty years. More than once, I've heard her say that her greatest happiness is finding a street in Manhattan where she had never walked. Thoreau says a similar thing about farms in Concord. At the end of his life, he was still finding ones he had never seen before, within walking distance of his house.

Because a walk is simultaneously forward in space and time— you are literally always walking away from yourself as you return to yourself—and also a heightening of consciousness, thinking while walking can enact both the recapturing of memories and the relinquishing of the past.

Here is something from near the beginning of one of the great Ginsberg poems written from the middle of his experience, drafted after staying up all night with a friend and talking and then walking home to his apartment in another neighborhood.

> No more to say, and nothing to weep for but the Beings in the Dream, trapped in its disappearance,
>
> sighing, screaming with it, buying and selling pieces of phantom, worshipping each other, worshipping the God included in it all— longing or inevitability?—while it lasts, a Vision—anything more?
>
> It leaps about me, as I go out and walk the street, look back over my shoulder, Seventh Avenue, the battlements of window office buildings shouldering each other high, under a cloud, tall as the sky an instant—and the sky above—an old blue place.
>
> or down the Avenue to the south, to—as I walk toward the Lower East Side—where you walked 50 years ago, little girl—from Russia,

eating the first poisonous tomatoes of America—frightened on the dock—

then struggling in the crowds of Orchard Street toward what?—toward Newark—toward candy store, first home-made sodas of the century, hand-churned ice cream in backroom on musty brownfloor boards—

Toward education marriage nervous breakdown, operation, teaching school, and learning to be mad, in a dream—what is this life?

Toward the Key in the window—and the great Key lays its head of light on top of Manhattan, and over the floor, and lays down on the sidewalk—in a single vast beam, moving, as I walk down First toward the Yiddish Theater—and the place of poverty you knew, and I know, but without caring now—Strange to have moved thru Paterson, and the West, and Europe and here again,

with the cries of Spaniards now in the doorstoops doors and dark boys on the street, fire escapes old as you

—Tho you're not old now, that's left here with me—

Myself, anyhow, maybe as old as the universe—and I guess that dies with us—enough to cancel all that comes—What came is gone forever every time—

That's good! That leaves it open for no regret—no fear radiators, lacklove, torture even toothache in the end—

The leaps of changing scenery encourage him to make sudden leaps in time. The leaps are also away from himself, into his mother's experience forty or fifty years earlier. When you walk, you do something that writers need to do to make their poems. You get out of your own way. You become less self-conscious. Maybe you get beyond your preconceived notions of yourself. Maybe you get to what you really care about.

This part of *Kaddish* may seem, like some of the poems by his friend Frank O'Hara, extremely literal in that he takes the conditions of the walk that in part jarred the poem loose and brings these impressions into the poem. When we look at less literal poems like Lorca's poems in *Poet in New York* and Neruda's "Walking Around," we may find that the walk has suggested a rhythm of perception and lineation rather than a sequence. According to the Ginsberg biography *Dharma Lion,* the second part of *Howl,* the Moloch section, was written after taking a lengthy walk in San Francisco. When he writes, "Moloch in whom I sit lonely," where he literally was sitting was in a coffee shop in the basement of a big hotel.

Obviously, most poems are not written due to the direct effects of physical exertions such as ambling around for a period of time, but when I read very long and discursive poems, I sometimes feel that the poet has different sort of inner, biological, lyric-sized clock, and this affects and lessens the energy of voice and sense of pacing. If I like it, there is some walking involved in there somehow anyway. The greatest value of walking for poets is that walks remind us what poems feel like, what it is like to breathe and be surprised by what comes next, to have one perception after another, to start out and to end up.

Jazz Vocalists, Other Vocalists, Poetry, and the Technologies of Voice

Home-made, home-made
    —Elizabeth Bishop

Used and Discount Records

Which do I like better, books or music? Glad I don't have to choose. Short form. My first weird album—as in, not actively pursued by another person in the house—was a late thirties Louis Armstrong compilation on the Joker label. My mother had it for "The Flat Foot Floogie," the Slim Gaillard song that Armstrong dropped with the Mills Brothers. Her 1940 rag doll on Decatur Avenue in the Bronx was named Flat Foot Floogie. I discovered this album, pressed by West Germans, in maybe 1983. It made me even weirder in seventh grade, liking that archaic stuff, "Jeepers Creepers," "Ain't Misbehaving," "West End Blues," and also "Strutting with Some Barbecue." There was a used bookstore where I bought the novels and stories that were the basis of the movies I liked—*From Here to Eternity* by the great James Jones, for instance, and *The Sweet Smell of Success and Other Stories* by Ernest Lehman, or *Rear Window and Other Stories* by Cornell Woolrich, old potboilers like *Anatomy of a Murder,* their soundtracks in my head. It had been my brother's favorite head shop and waterbed emporium before this lady Toba Levinson bought it and turned it into a bookstore. I often wondered if this happened because her son, like my own brother, was a head, and she wanted for her boy to stop buying bongs. I don't think this was the case. There were still a few racy touches. She sold postcards like the one with the black and white photo of an ancient topless woman and a banner that read "Strutting with Some Barbecue." I can't remember if the photo showed her working a big open grill and wearing a chef's hat or if she were merely displaying a wide platter of ribs.

Introducing one shredding exchange between himself and the rhythm section, Armstrong says, "Boys, get your chops together. I'm coming over there after you." Then he sings,

> *What is this thing*
> *called Swing?*

More openly transgressing. More sweet. Popcorn. Butter. Pizza. Candy bars. Turkish Nibs. Coca-Cola. Pain. Mountain Dew. Love. Dough.

First off, I want to say that when you clear away the scholarship of one and the drunk mannerisms of the other, a lot about the relationship between American music and poetry can be derived from *Blues People* and *Black Music* by Amiri Baraka and scattered comments by Jack Kerouac, who gets too little respect for all that people sincerely love him, about his method of composition, particularly when he dwells on phrases and clauses as breath units, working in the spirit of Pound's ideas about really musical writing in "A Retrospect." It is better to get this from the music itself or from rummaging around in *Transbluesency.* I like to mix and match. When I moved to Massachusetts twenty years ago, I remember hearing Robert Pinsky and thinking, "That guy is a saxophone when he gets going." His ideas about poetry as a technology in itself certainly felt demonstrated by his own musicality. Then I would hear David Rivard read poems like "The Debt" from *Wise Poison,* and think, "That guy is a saxophone, too. So different." I remember seeing a Boston poet named Bill Corbett's face turn into an upturned, golden bell as he read a poem with a lot of names in it to about ten people at the New England Institute of Art. This didn't require much explaining to myself or recourse to much of my vocabulary.

I always felt suspect about the way that I loved vocalists, all of them. Dumb thing to feel suspect about. Even if there were something off about words and other vocals, they would still lead to the instrumentals, and those are vocals too. A cursory listening to Thelonious Monk play "Bemsha Swing" or Coltrane's *Lush Life* should be enough to prepare anybody for the sentence structures of the first pages of *Moby Dick*. Somehow, without ever hearing anybody say anything about her, I managed to find a Billie Holiday album. Some funky cheap label, early seventies or late sixties, I guess, looking at the cover. The same summer I also bought the brand-new *Standing on the Beach* album by the Cure. Made cassette tapes of both of them, walked endlessly on the beach. Bought the Holiday album for two dollars—I still have it and enjoy it—from a used-record shop that was located, incongruously in the basement of an office building where there was also a Middle Eastern restaurant and a dress shop that seemed to be full of pink tulle, an old lady standing in a ten-by-ten glass box surrounded by mirrors and dresses, her mouth full of pins.

Horrible influence on me, that album. The one that really freaked me out—though none of the songs were within my frame of reference except a swingy "Them There Eyes"—was "I Cover the Waterfront." What was that supposed to mean? She was some sort of cop or heartbroken person looking for somebody who had committed the crime of breaking her heart. Maybe she meant like fog, some sort of big feeling of herself turned to fog.

I am happy that at that point, I did not discover Dave Brubeck or something. I might have ended up the Vice Principal who decides how long kids get suspended for at the tech high school, or maybe this time you just turn them over to the cops. That's what happened to Paul Ryan. It wasn't just Ayn Rand. It was bad music. Who cares what he listens to while he lifts weights with his lackeys? It seems high-school music teachers are always saying, "I teach them jazz." Maybe that's not true. I am pretty sure that even Bob Jones University has a college jazz band. Writers should know better.

The next one I loved was Ella Fitzgerald. She was the bells.

Say, I don't mean to interrupt myself and all these fond memories of the archaic technologies of voice, but there was a time in my early twenties when my friend Ken Selig and I would get together every Sunday night and go out to hear live music. Saturday was not enough for us. We needed to get nice and ready for the week. Often, like some Jerry Lewis character, I would wait tables on Sundays. Had this gig at Kiku, the Japanese restaurant. Got to wear a short maroon Japanese coat, vaguely inappropriate for serving sushi, and a tie, but it looked sharp. I had a navy blue one with a big abstract-looking kanji character or something on the back. I didn't trouble myself figuring that out. I would like to go back in time as a wiser person mostly. The bartender Larry called it "the snowflake jacket." The waitresses called him *Tanuki,* which maybe helped him calm down. Raccoon dog. Ken hadn't gone back to school yet and become the worldwide head of all IT helpdesks for an insurance company or whatever it is the French pay him to do in that skyscraper in Manhattan. He was selling cameras and lenses at the camera store on Forbes Avenue in Squirrel Hill—the ancient shop with a neon camera blinking in its sign over the sidewalk, the kind where the bulb falls out of the metal dish on it.

Why was he doing this?

"Well, I know I feel kind of grouchy once in awhile, but really I think of myself as a people person. What? Why are you laughing? I am."

So every Sunday night, we would go to a jazz club. There were at most five or six places in the entire city of Pittsburgh where you could hear jazz, always at irregular hours such as at brunch, but this was the best, a bar so beautiful everything tasted and sounded even better. The headliners were a singer and a trombone player. I liked to watch the singer demolish a few plates of appetizers before going on. She went on hard. Pre-game meal. "On Green Dolphin Street," but first, the beef tartare, pre-Atkins Diet.

Around this time, my brother was a big Deadhead, and some of my roommates in college were junior-grade Deadheads. They liked to listen to the endless versions of "Dancing in the Street" recorded with a disco beat in various corners of America on cassette tape, occasionally emerging from a cloud of pot smoke to announce, in all seriousness, "This is just like jazz." Something about the late middle-aged scene on a Sunday night in Pittsburgh, hearing the musicians eat their wings, made me think that there was something indefinite about that statement. Even today, when I describe a long boring poem or poetic sequence as a jam-band poem, I am not sending them the full compliments of Garcia. It's more of a West Coast thing to me, all that time driving around, too much time on the bus, not enough on their feet.

The first Ella Fitzgerald album I came across was a remaindered-bin, Italian import of her late '30s and early '40s singles, stuff like "Paper Moon" and "Mr. Paganini" and "A-Tisket, A-Tasket" and the song with the Ink Spots, "Cow Cow Boogie." I snagged this at the University of Pittsburgh Book Store along with an Italian Lou Reed. I perhaps played Ella for my brother, and hearing the lyrics about "he was raised on loco weed," my brother may have said, "See. See." And then it was off to rummage in his cigar box of bootleg cassettes to get the best "Fire on the Mountain"; you know, the one from the truck-stop roller derby in Flagstaff, Arizona, in 1979, when Jerry was back from rehab but not through tripping. That album did me okay for about two years. The next Ella album I stumbled upon was one of her Verve Songbook albums, *The Cole Porter Songbook*. On the cover, Ella wears a matronly dress. She looks like she owns several strands of expensive pearls and croons in pink and blue panels of color, a beautifully heavy double album held together by a plastic sleeve. I bought this in a walk-up used-record store down by the colleges after doing worse than all of my practice tests would have projected on the SATs, which I took at the last possible moment surrounded by Central Catholic football players who were stomping their work boots with anger all around the room. I had cut so much school that I wasn't even kidding myself. One of the best things about music is that it suspends time as it works with it. I knew all about suspensions.

Even earlier, even more of a kid, when I listened to Frank Sinatra in escapist reverie like an overweight and sluggishly sixth-grade bobby-soxer, I would write the lyrics out as he sang them on one of those pads pharmaceutical reps were always giving my mother at the clinic. I think this is because there were so many senior citizens— good company for a loner—on my paper route. I would figure out where the breaks would go, try to make it like the Beatles albums with the lyrics printed on the sleeve. I think this is my earliest experience with the line. What the hell was I doing? Coming upon the pad, my brother was impressed. He thought I had written the maudlin lyrics to "Young at Heart." Or maybe it was "All the Way," which Bob Dylan discovers with his whispery torch like some sort of cave painting of an antelope hunt on his new album, *Fallen Angels.* So the first feedback I received as a writer was utterly spurious. Get used to it, kid. You can go work in the poetry fields.

Cassette Tapes

In college, my Ella album was *Clap Hands, Here Comes Charlie,* a great and bluesy album of torch songs with spare arrangements she recorded in the early sixties. I bought the cassette cheap at the National Record Mart in Pittsburgh as the chain went out of business to listen to on my Walkman on the Amtrak back to New York. I had a very strange experience with this album, listening to it a few times a week in my apartment on Hoffman Street in the Bronx, a walk-up above a social club where a gangster of some standing used to hang out in his silvery suits, happy to talk about Plato because he had studied philosophy at Lehman College. I spent a bit more time with this gentleman than I would have liked, as I had bounced my rent check and had to make nightly repayments out of my waiter money to the bartender, a huge and somber man with a big guy ponytail. When I would fork over my forty or eighty or one hundred dollars, he would give me a beer on the house, and several times I saw him put Michael Bolton on the juke box, and behind the bar, he would stride back and forth, mouthing the lyrics to "How Am I Supposed to Live Without You." This sounded funny if I made him into another Michael Bolton joke, but it moved me as a terrible revelation of deceived self-conception. Tone reads us. Then the gangster would buy me another beer, and he would ask me questions about how I had bounced the check, which he found grim and bemusing. "But you are paying it back, kid. You are doing things right for now. What do you think of this guy, Euthyphro?" Or he would say, "Pittsburgh. Hmmmm. That's out west. That's further west." At the end of the summer, he offered to help me pay for law school.

Shaken by these happenings and nursing my own moody heartbreak, I would return to my foldable IKEA desk and listen to Ella sing about how "spring can really hang you up the most" on my boom box. Late July, the fire hydrants were often open to cool the kids off, fat boy dragged through the whitewater rush by his foot so he would not swallow all that soft water from upstate you drink in the apartments.

All that bartender needed was a microphone. He was a vocalist too. He had an air microphone. That fall, my whole family came back to New York for Thanksgiving. The day after Thanksgiving, we went for drinks in a place in SoHo—a neighborhood name my father and his brothers rejected like the legitimacy of the Mets compared to their vanished Giants and Dodgers, and Vince Scully moved to California—where the tables seemed to each have a heavy red velvet curtain around them, like a sort of hospital of pleasure. There was a singer, impressively slinky, a redhead in a black dress, and she entranced me and perturbed me by singing several of the songs from *Clap Hands, Here Comes Charlie* note for note, a compelling payer of tributes. Though I had not read "The Work of Art in the Age of Mechanical Reproduction," the gap created was perhaps lesson number one. The gap is when you decide for a moment the Lincoln Center Jazz Orchestra is worth hearing or not, when you think maybe institutions can swing a bit, or maybe you better get out of the gap.

The Technologies of Voice

"Tune in this time to another episode of the jazz in my head." Doesn't everybody think that? Or hasn't everybody thought that?

Apparently, no. Most of the language I'm hearing these days seems to come with no demand at all except the Elvis demand: "Love me." Actually, something that clearly wanting is rare in itself. My favorite moment in a Louise Glück poem is a non-dramatic moment in a lyric. She is riding the subway with an Otis Redding album in her lap, valuable, kind of bulky, off to listen to it by herself for love, which she remembers.

It's okay, you know, that people go to school for jazz. They would anyway, one way or another. You can hear all sorts of music-school musicians at Wally's Cafe in Boston, and they sound good making music that is always changing. Nobody gets on visual artists for getting art training, unlike writers and musicians. A drunken Vietnam vet turned novelist once turned to me and several other graduate student types at a writer's conference bar-side ATM and snorted happily at us and his own big, one-off publishing contract. "You all go to graduate school for writing, like going to college to learn to fuck." It was true. He could have been Billy Eckstine to me there in Pittsburgh, hometown of Ahmad Jamal and Gerald Stern, but I was partially annoyed anyway.

Speaking that way, one thing I decided early on was I don't like when even very good poets sing or even warble at readings, not even when they are quoting song lyrics. You know, in the middle of poems, all of a sudden, it's a question. "Is this supposed to sound like Tony Bennett? It doesn't." My friend Natalie can sing. The greatest and most expressive poet to do this embarrassing thing would have to be Allen Ginsberg, who even went around with a little keyboard. Perhaps because I have a streak of lousy in me, I don't like being reminded of the poet in the middle of a poem, his or her neediness for admiration, even sympathy, all poking through and getting in the way of the poem, not unless that is what the poems do, too. Then it's impolite *not* to feel moved because I feel the vibration in the air of something repeated and allowed in advance, ugh, disturbing.

Maybe the reason I like New England is people walk around looking down at the ground, and this gives them a certain gravity, always looking at their feet. Then they get startled by some happy eye contact, and it is more meaningful. "Hey, it's a beautiful night."

"Yes, you have a beautiful night, too."

Then the man smiles, and he didn't when people thanked him for hitting their driveway with his snow-blower. That level of uncomprehending loneliness is the hallmark of the natural person each one of us actually is. One of the best teachers I ever had is this great poet from around Boston, Alan. He told me the worst poetry reading of his entire life was this famous poet, and she read for two hours. Then she took out a guitar and sang with an Irish accent, and she was neither Irish nor a singer. Then she read some translations. Then she read her students' poems. And then some more of her poems, and one by a prisoner. I'm probably making some of this up. Then she sang some more. He about died. The truck from the funny farm is going to get Alan, if you make him hear you think you can sing again. Put down that guitar. I hope he wasn't in the front row. Poetry is not so intellectual after all. It is more of a series of physical responses. I don't want to typecast him as an impatient fellow, which would be far from the truth.

Somebody like Alan is the audience inside the audience with a better stereo system, and so with different needs, as my friend likes to say. I think most poets feel the same way though, no matter what they cop to feeling for social reasons. The real testy ones do not even like a poet to say anything between poems perhaps because they believe that art after jazz should involve some suffering on the part of the audience. You start singing to some of these somber avant-garde characters, and you will get a note from their doctor cautioning you about excessive displays of the wrong kind of humanness. They give you permission to read with your back to the audience and emulate a pissed-off Miles Davis. And people all over New England, no matter what their background or even if they are immigrants here, say, five years if not sooner, if not right away, they will give you the moon so long as you don't seem needy. Most of us treasure those moments of being in it and out of it at the same time. I don't know if that's my surroundings or poetry. If you unpack this bag, you wind up thinking the singer is more important than the song, and that, for me, is lead in the water, but please be a human being, too, and if you must go wrong, go wrong in that direction.

Vanities of poets, some of them are sweet. I don't think any of mine are, involved as they are more in my dislikes than in my likings. One of them has to do with ideas about music, and of thinking of ourselves as inspired singers, some of us with that weird humming going for something entirely vatic instead of trusting voice. I believe we are influenced by singers. According to Gary Giddins, when Bing Crosby was a jazz singer early on, working with a guitar player named Eddie Lang and listening to Louis Armstrong as Louis Armstrong was listening to him, Crosby was really inventing singing with the microphone with startling suave intimacy and lightning quick invention. The vocalists followed the instrumentalists who were already playing expressive syntax and sentence structure, but they all got even better after that. And really poets of the voice come after the microphone being discovered as such an intimate tool, and not just obviously Frank O'Hara and "Personism" but the subtle and plain-spoken lot of American poetry which begins not with oratorical Whitman, but Williams in his small poems' rapid fire, more tonal moves—not only precipitous shifts of collaged diction—than had happened in any compact lyric poems, at least those written in English. The French may have anticipated the record player.

Without the record albums of jazz and pop, would Williams have been such a strong influence? This kinship does not make us singers or fully musicians. Maybe it makes us vocalists. Though I am not about to convert my anthologies into doorstops, most everything before, say, Elizabeth Bishop and Philip Larkin sounds positively blown into a megaphone in terms of tonal expressiveness and play by comparison. Bishop was listening to Billie Holiday use the microphone live and on records. What does Bashō say? Don't emulate the old poets, but go for what they wanted. People around here walk around like hard-ass judges when they are not bumbling around like shy characters between the graves of Henry and William James. I do, too. This is partially comical, partially insane, but it has its wintry charm, and there are a lot of good times. Record stores live.

Anonymous Raincoats—Later Poetry of Seamus Heaney and Tomaž Šalamun in Translation

Do you like American music?
We like all kinds of music.
                    —The Violent Femmes

—You must be a prizefighter.
—No, I'm a shamus.
                    —*The Big Sleep* (1946)

When it came out about a year after his death, I loved the second *Selected Heaney,* the one spanning the last twenty-five years of his life, 1988–2013. Almost all of those later books, I read as they appeared, generally thinking that they were not as good as the earlier work, but that maybe I was wrong. Reading them together, you realize how wise Heaney was about separating himself from the influences of self-consciousness. You can talk about later Heaney and early Heaney, and the voice in the poems is utterly different. The second Heaney is a master of internal exile coming home. And he feels more improvisational, though that manner may be protective coloration for his genius.

In her essay on *The Haw Lantern* in *Soul Says,* a now-"of its time" book of essays, Helen Vendler takes a poem in that collection as a sign of things to come beyond it, and she wonders what "a poetry of airy listening" would be like. It turns out to be earthy and resistant to rhetoric. Like the older William Carlos Williams, Heaney becomes pastoral and epic, at least through translation, but he also writes poems that are the opposite of self-impressed, weird and funky incantatory poems, and even poems with awful jokey sides to them as well, like "The Butts."

At Fordham in 1990, where he was the first poet I ever heard, Heaney told the students that his mother had taught him to prefer a plain wooden spoon for a child's toy rather than a plastic beach shovel that would break, an image that I found haunting, and had nothing to compare it to at the time. It is not often you hear a metaphor, really, not even at a Jesuit school. The McGinley Lecture, I believe. Rivard compares him to Bashō. In an Art of Poetry interview in *The Paris Review,* Heaney remembers Williams seeming to offer "a music that stopped exactly where the line stopped. No resonance, no back echo, no canorous note." This seems like a good description of how Heaney's later tone sounds, but the explicators will not go hungry for want of subject matter. I think Heaney would have liked to go incognito in his raincoat like Williams, or just among friends. He certainly didn't let anybody put him on a t-shirt. This is suggested by many retiring moments in his poems, even an early one, "Oracle."

From early on, Heaney had a sense that a culture was something at least in part to fend off. The thing I want to think about—Heaney's relationship to American poetry—is difficult because Heaney, in his deepest resources when he speaks about what did and did not influence his art, is defensive. He protects his sources, or maybe he tried not to give them more thought than would have been useful for him. We see this when he complains, in *The Government of the Tongue,* about the "ironic younger poets of England and America." For a long time, I tried to figure out who he was talking about. All I kept meeting were believers in witness, dogged grief, and traumatized survivors. Poetry lovers and poets are some of the most powerfully earnest people in the world. When Heaney does talk about American poets and poetry, he is mainly writing with affection for certain social connections, mentioning people he respects and loves, people who encouraged him by being excellent in themselves, and kind to him. He remembers givers; the mid-stride poet of *The Haw Lantern* has a pious side, and though by the time he wrote this book, he was spending more time in America, he seems less influenced by the version of American poetry that seems most authentic to me. This is not to say that there are not deep affinities between, for instance, "Mycenae Lookout" and Frank Bidart's dramatic monologues, or that he underrated the poets whose work he heard in America, the community of poets he obviously loved, or anything like that.

Even so, Heaney seems most vitally influenced by American poetry right *before* he regularly taught here. It could be that American poetry itself became more responsible and civic at the same time that Heaney did. It could also be that Heaney was just very busy responding to student work while he toiled here. Teaching Heaney's second and third books in an introduction to poetry class over a number of semesters, reading his greatest stuff, namely the poems in *North,* along with *The Branch Will Not Break* by James Wright, where I did not expect to find connections to Heaney, and Theodore Roethke's *The Lost Son and Other Poems,* where I expected to find more than a love-mud feeling, but didn't really, it occurred to me that my favorite Heaney has lot more in common with James Wright's damaged, associative, leaping, politically resonant pastorals that remain musical and even metrical while loosening music, than the American poets whom Heaney actually mentions, and that includes Frost and Roethke. After his second book of pronouncements about poetry and the poems in *Field Work,* another high-water mark, Heaney was aiming at something as true and as responsible as the super-nobility of the Polish poets in confronting evil with humility and a dazzling subtly that made him feel like a stumbling school boy haunting the ruin of a Norman tower in "The Master," a Sweeney-themed poem in *Station Island,* another all-around clock-cleaner.

When you move from Heaney's first three books to *North,* there is a huge and somewhat anomalous shift in his technique. This shift is one of the great moments in twentieth-century poetry, comparable to the leap made by Merwin—another no-show in Heaney's prose, but in fact an inescapable figure—for us, at least—while writing *The Moving Target* to the sorts of poetry that would lead him to *The Lice,* or when Wright, encouraged by Bly, ceased to be a fifties formalist. How does this happen? How do we go from "Follower" to "Punishment"?

23

There is a sonnet that forms a tribute to Billie Holiday to answer a ghoulish cover version of the Dubliners' bloody and macho rebel song, "Will You Come to the Bower?" I would say that American poetry has quite a lot to do with it. Heaney actually wrote lyrics for a song that the Dubliners did not record. They were one of the bands that Shane McGowan from the Pogues found punky in his diaspora public housing hells in his teenage London. There is great footage of the Pogues and the Dubliners joining forces to do the moonshine song "Mountain Dew" on television, and both bands having a ball. It's nothing like the embarrassed Ramones playing with Sha-Na-Na, except in optics.

In *Stepping Stones* and other places as well, Heaney attributes this amazing development—the jump to *North* and away from the conventional poetics of Belfast—to a few things in his living circumstances. One was chain-smoking like W. H. Auden up in his thatch. One was a move to a year teaching at Berkeley, his first move out of the north. At Berkeley, Heaney purchased large stacks of used American poetry books and heard a number of anti-war readings, where the passionate moral certainty of Snyder and Bly reminded him of moralistic Protestant ministers. This is one of those moments when Heaney freely owns that he has a version of a European Catholic moral nature. He feels morally compromised by and complicit in whatever ails the world. Here and elsewhere, he speaks of American poetry as something that was not very easy for him to hear and grasp as poetry and which he admired in strikingly hard-won but somewhat limited ways. He also says, surprisingly, that he got a stronger grasp on Yeats there. I wonder if that means "Lapis Lazuli" sounded better in California. Yeats is a big leaper. And then there was his move to Wicklow, closer to the serenity of his imagined childhood. Heaney points out that he was moving in certain directions that he took in *North* before he came to America.

In other words, Heaney didn't need to go to Berkeley to write "Bogland." If there is an American influence here, it is Lowell's sort of social poetry mixed with soft-downward-sigh personal sensation and journalistic details. But he may have needed to go to Berkeley, and to hear the crazy runs and jumps of Bay Area poets and voices, to write "Viking Dublin: Trial Pieces," a poem of Irish jazz, one that embraces the conditions of its own making, in the manner of much American poetry, music and visual art. To see what I mean, take both poems down off the shelf and read them aloud to yourself, and please, American poetry lovers, even if you have a degree in Irish Studies from Boston College, no fake Irish accents. The dead can hear you. Don't embarrass yourself in front of them. You will feel the Lowell of *Life Studies* and *For the Union Dead* and *Near the Ocean* in the elegant "Bogland." But when you get to "Viking Dublin: Trial Pieces" and past the giant Irish nose "sniffing" down the Liffey—a nice Monty Python cut-out animation, there—you will find that this poem of "trial pieces, / the craft's mystery / improvised on bone" is not just about the Viking side of Irishness. It is is also about jive-talking in general. The poem sounds even better, and more like itself, if you drop the numbers and read through the section breaks. Heaney even gets some Sinatra in there:

(DO NOT TRY TO SOUND IRISH)

Come fly with me,
come sniff the wind
with the expertise
of the Vikings—

neighborly, scoretaking
killers, haggers,
and haggler, gombeen-men,
hoarders of grudges and gain.

With a butcher's aplomb
they spread out your lungs
and made you warm wings
for your shoulders.

Old fathers, be with us.
Old cunning assessors
of feuds and of sites
for ambush or town.

(SECTION BREAK, DO NOT SAY 6)

"Did you ever hear tell,"
said Jimmy Farrell
"of the skulls they have
in the city of Dublin?

And so on. Later, the poem gets even better. Imagine some old raggedy character saying as they shove her into the squad car, "My words lick around / cobbled quays, go hunting / lightly as pampooties / over the skull-capped ground, Sweetie." *Sweetie* is not in the poem, but I think you should know that it is. When I was in Ireland a few years ago, I made sure to visit some of these trial pieces in the Viking Room at the Irish National Museum. There they were amid cases of rusty swords and dioramas of Viking Dublin: such small, out-of-the-way, unlikely objects upon which to spring such great poetry, little pieces of New Bedford Whaling Museum scrimshaw upstairs from the ancient gold of the jewelry and the Cross of Cong. Apparently, he had seen a larger selection of them, but truly, on the basis of this selection, Heaney was always the master of the wooden spoon. See Heaney coming here, slapping on his black cat bone, picking up on some other parts of folk modernism. Our own engagement with our entire lives should be as good.

I lived in Ireland for a year when I was a grade-school kid. I'm second-generation and Catholic, but with a Presbyterian Antrim grandfather who converted. My late mother wasn't Irish. She just wanted to be. When she was still in her early thirties, she even dyed her hair red to match her five freckled babies. Hybrid comes easy to me, but I know that I write with a dented helmet of American-ness around my head. We lived south of Dublin, towards Wicklow, where

Heaney lived in the country, and now there is a Texaco Station where there used to be a suburban cow pasture down the block from our old house. The Irish National Museum has its own bog people now, or at least parts of them, on display. If you visit Ceide Fields on the cliffs in north Mayo, there is a movie in the visitors' center that begins with Heaney reading a poem about the place from *North*. While Yeats owns the Irish myths, Heaney, a great observer, accompanies the postmodern archeologist. No doubt a lot of Irish people would roll their eyes at this as "a bunch of bleeding stones, big bleeding deal," as my friend, a cable-television installer from Limerick, puts it. Wedge tombs were not a thing in the seventies.

Thanks to the EU, you can buy kielbasa and Polish sardines and instant white borscht in old County Mayo market towns my grandmother knew. Poland and Ireland are near of kin. I saw that, and I still felt at home. My wife's hometown. New Britain, Connecticut. Broad Street. Polish Hill. Pittsburgh. Worcester. The world. I like these short Irish guys who marry tall Polish women. You can meet these couples in airports.

All that aside, I once had a dream after hearing Heaney give a lecture during the second Bush administration. He was sitting on some logs in a state park, and he had a crushed Mountain Dew can coming out of his forehead and some cobwebs, like his head was turning into some kind of log as well, partially eaten away by termites. That's what it was like to think about Heaney during the second Iraq War. I think he really was disgusted with us. It made me feel sadder than few dreams I have ever had. *Look what you're doing to me. And to everybody. You terrible people. All you want to hear about is frogspawn.* My God, I thought, Seamus Heaney maybe hates us. On some level, Iowa is his idea of snowstorms from hell. Why would Heaney write about a snowstorm in Iowa? Part of the answer is simple. Bush. We sort of elected him.

During the second Bush administration and the Clinton years, the European godfather of younger American poetry with a charge of being unforeseen was the Slovenian poet, Tomaž Šalamun. Unhampered by excessive fame or any noisy interest in his own country here, he saw America and younger American poetry as soil well prepared for his own adventurous streak by Frank O'Hara and John Ashbery. Here is the poem "manhattan" from *A Ballad for Metka Krašovec,* written perhaps in 1980 but not making itself felt until we needed to be reminded of it—

> I'm crucified
> Between continents.
> Between loves.
> My nests are in the air.
> They burn with a gentle flame.
> A white sail hides me from
> photographers, Hudson River.
> The water is deeper here.
> The sky a darker gray.
> On the horizon
> two blunt pencils.
> Dug in,
> I won't be coming home.
> (trans. by Michael Biggins)

The perverse image of the crucifix here is also love with open arms. When he goes to see Woody Allen's *Manhattan,* he jumps up in his seat and applauds all the disreputable freedom, stays, and then watches the movie again. No need to justify any kind of humanness, certainly not decadence, for Šalamun.

Šalamun is one of those poets who remind you that your disreputable resources are not only your best ones, but also the ones that you have to burn, your language, love, and freedom. In all of the books of translations of his work, there are some mighty boring sections, but never a single moment that feels composed by the superego to demonstrate righteousness, to display learning for the sake of learning, or to demonstrate skill without occasion. Like Simic, he was a great truant, an imaginative way out of social and familial dilemmas, responsibilities, bystanding, traditional versification, headshot marketing, and the dulling influence of believing that lyric poetry and narrative essays are basically the same thing, some cement shoes. In addition to being brilliant and weird, Šalamun also had trauma cachet, *bonus alibi,* the seriousness of the world he let in, an equally dark historical sense of Europe, but less, or almost none, of the guilt, and connections to the more glamorous worlds of visual art than Heaney's deep engagement with folk music, oh no ("The Singer's House"). Heaney's reaction, if he had had one, may have been to say, "Phew. That's a few less books to sign. Get away from me, kids. You bother me." And Helen Vendler didn't write about his work, and neither did Marjorie Perloff probably, an enormous plus for many lovers of the secret art. Cosmopolitan, an identity and an anti-identity at once, at home in the city and in the countryside, sexual, and privileging nothing, T. S. went elegantly back and forth between Europe and America, too, almost the dream of Bob Dylan, perfectly anonymous, perfectly strange and individual. Of course, none of this might have been true for the poets who actually studied with Heaney at Harvard or for poets seeking traditional formal mastery.

When I moved to Boston twenty years ago, not sure if I wanted to be very noble or not, and not aware of many poets who were mixing registers, but wanting to find them, Heaney had recently won the Nobel Prize. The way people liked Heaney seemed to be unhealthy for poets with a feeling for public intellectual life, somehow. There was too much love of virtue in it, a desire for the superego to do too much of the job. Most were not getting Heaney's heat, just his beautiful ethics. In graduate school, formal revivalists had an annoying love of Heaney, too, like bullies loving something good. They were anvil-heads, too. The anvil is a Robert Graves image for meter in *The Crowning Privilege,* and when Heaney calls out some of his critics for their "anvil brains," he is saying something about believers in formal rigidity in his own neighborhood. Tracy K. Smith says, "I wanted to be Seamus Heaney" because of his generous teaching and his first book. As a reader, I felt something similar, along with just about everybody else just starting to write or study poetry then. How long was this line to get *Seeing Things* signed going to be anyway?

For a lot of younger poets, maybe even twenty years of American poets by now, Heaney has become hard to see—less necessary—for his academic admirers' temperate enthusiasms, a canonical fate. That Walcott gets largely ignored by this small but always growing constituency seems even crazier when one actually reads *The Schooner Flight* (big enough for italics, and few poems should be bigger), *Sea Grapes,* and *The Arkansas Testament.* However, as poetry means space for unique sensibility, voice and intimacy, the best time to read anybody is when his or her or their reputation is somewhat obscure, whether waxing or waning. It is getting possible to find ourselves in Heaney again, to encounter the bodily word. I'm talking about poetry and consciousness. St. Seamus the Respectable and Correct was probably no fun for Seamus Heaney, the unself-conscious poet, even if he was glad that his version of Sophocles, and his poetry in general, helped inspire good things, like Bill Clinton helping the peace process or Joe Biden giving a better speech, good things personally, too, no doubt. By the way, in *Stepping Stones,* after hemming and hawing a bit about the Lewinsky scandal, Heaney concludes, "I supported Bill, and I support Hillary, too."

My favorite Heaney remains the anti-Heaney in Heaney, or as I like to think of him, the Heaney in plain sight who jokes about fiddle-heads, and who makes jokes about the Pennines and dead moles, the bawdy translator of *The Midnight Report,* and oysters, the one who felt like "an old pike all badged with sores / wanting to swim in touch with soft-mouthed life." I suppose this is another name for the counterweighting Shameless Heiney loved by all eternal students. As all great poems of shared life can be said to be co-authored, he also co-authored a great love poem, "The Skunk."

As for my favorite Heaney poem, "The Harvest Bow" is written with silence for an Irish father in that common language, roots-y and rooted in raw love period, realistic and un-pretty, and beautiful, a poem that seems to combine all of the ways we love Seamus Heaney in one. It's a perfect magic spell, and Heaney was a mage at his best. I have no idea what it is like to read Osip Mandelstam in Russian, but our language has this consolation in it. The poem even has cockfighting and an outhouse in it, an old bed in the weeds. "The end of art is peace / could be the motto of this frail device." Maybe that *could be* implies the end of art is not just peace. Surely, it implies *should be.* A lot of art is dull, old Father Auden knew, and all poets dull when taken in excessive quantity. Bless page limits. In any case, the poetry is "burnished by its passing and still warm." Now that he is completely beyond our fashions, we can find Heaney again, a different one who was always there, if we can hear tone, always a big if.

ODE TO MENTALITY, OR POETRY NEEDS WEIRD SUBJECTIVITY

I'm working for free. I'm not a cynic.
—Alan Dugan

… one discovers in it after all, a place for the genuine.
—Marianne Moore

An Image for Readers

"Does this poet just have an institutional imagination?"

That is the big question you ask when you read a poem, if you go looking for something genuine. "Or is this one maybe, like me, sort of crouched over here behind that garbage can across the street?" Hiding from trouble, or just waiting on it? Then, if you are lucky, you sort of look over there, appreciatively, see an elbow behind that bent number with a Yard Waste sticker peeling across it. "It looks like this one really does mean some kind of business."

Maybe this poet even turns bright blue, like certain species of poisonous tree frogs. Or a bunch of hands start waving around her body, a fine bit of special effects, simple stagecraft (Ginger Rogers) or something inexplicable (Ginger Rogers). Maybe this character, whom you have realized does not have an institutional imagination after all, and who probably does not exist, just stands there, in no way intending to watch you start in on your skit, on your parody, snapping your fingers, taking your solo. "When you're a Jet, you're a Jet all the way." This one might have written one chapbook, kind of surreal and/or twee, and now their new work is strictly documentarian, one image and bit after another, followed by chortles and sobs, with other sections making you aware of the perversity of language, all these choices you might, given the choice to think about them for yourself, not even consider, but that does not mean they do not create a series of possibilities in which the possibility canceling out any possibility always remains a tragic possibility. What you will learn in any real poem is the story within the mere narrative, by way of inflection and trust. If a car pulls up, and the people in that car want to start some business, I know that a poet will weigh in, with words, possibly demonstrating something moral. In any of these scenarios, the effect can be called unsettling. All those eyes in the firkins in "Directive" are in fact other poets. Another possibility is that she is with the people in the car, on Twitter with every other broadcaster.

On the other hand, a diabolically bad poet is like a rotting corpse. You almost have to seek them out, dig around, Eyegore-like, for Dr. Frankenstein. There is also a poetry of real anger. You can't mess with real anger. It's hard to counterfeit real anger, but if an institutional poet or product, a good student of some sort, gets angry, you can tell because the meeting notes have angry coffee rings all over them. I mean you can see these things in the air like thought bubbles in a comic strip. The search for themes. If you get stuck feeling like that, you should go do stuff for work. It wears off if you take a walk. In itself, writing poetry is not even a subject. Free behavior depends on where a poet can find a peculiar form of mental life. There are free spirits everywhere, too, of every stripe and genre. But are there fewer of them? I think maybe so.

The Era of Various Spectrums

The era of some version of the campus pirate is thankfully long past at this point, I hope. Maybe we met some of these jolly Rogers when the grey hairs touched their temples in previous decades. Twenty-five years ago, at least one friend had at least one professor trying to French-kiss her against bookcases. That guy was old then. He must be ancient now, shirt tucked into his shorts. He remembers my friend. He says, "Arrgghh." Enough of him. Thank God for the overhaul of some institutional values. If it's the past we're talking about, we will have to use our imaginations to get free and even. Think of what Dugan says at the end of "The Jack-Off of the Graveyard Shift":

> Later
> the foreman said the cops
> had been around the office after him. He was
> a total innocent, a total fuck-up,
> a natural for the graveyard shift
> to liven up the nights of noise,
> with the four-slide stamping-out machines
> going 12-to-8, 12-to-8, 12-to-8,
> sex-and-money, sex-and-money, sex-and money.
> He was missed. He kept people from going crazy too.
> These stories were told about him for months.

Dugan's poem is full of non-institutional humanity. It seems like he was the last public defender who still believed in the insanity defense, and that we actually enjoy the story when somebody gets crazy sometimes, especially at a fortunate remove. You don't get moral credit for being better behaved than a crazy person trying to hump your leg while you keep the break-room coffee from burning your fingers. Yesterday's institutional imagination is sometimes tomorrow's sicko. Narratives of selfhood, overt or not, are more often than not big bores, same as anything else we attempt, attempts to guard and preserve the self from the risk of change, sometimes through the preservation of pain itself through narrative piety.

One of the more volatile elements you can add to poetry, requiring a novelist's cheerful honesty about the disreputable tactics each competitive self employs to blot out the claims of other people and imaginative observation rather than journalism, is social texture. Poets sometimes leave a lot of themselves out, and thus the anarchy of social texture gets left out of poems, even from social poems. It takes time to learn how to see, but some poets never bother with imagery, and they feel good. Nice introduction, lousy portfolio. Some prefer self-protective seriousness or even a sense of aesthetic mission, which often amount to the same thing, and some prefer *Don Juan*. It turns out that Byron is perhaps the more renewable, the far looser resource. Self-righteousness adds to greenhouse gas.

One recent academic year containing the start of a disastrous presidential election season ending in Trump got off to a bad start when an obscure poet and library professional pretended to be a Chinese lady named Yi-Fen Chou to get even more of his foursquare poems published. This was the first sour blast of the election season for poets—a season that would feature dirty tricks, false identities, scandals, racist and sexist attacks, resentment of intellectual elites and social structures, as well as outraged responses. The sheer insult and insensitivity made everybody feel terrible or irate. All that being the case, the next largely unspoken thing I think many poets felt is that making people self-conscious about their relationship to market conditions while they try to write poetry is just cruel. What other country do we have? I don't know what the poet's intentions were in this horrible remake of *Tootsie*—I am sure that I read something about *Tootsie*—maybe by the Wabash River in Indiana, feeding his pet goose under a troll bridge. No matter what the insult, and no matter the source of the insult, whether from within ourselves or from the system or from other individuals, the only way out of thinking defensively is to possess a core of subjective and idiosyncratic art and to blithely ignore or consume that which increases self-consciousness and market thought, the enemies of creative generosity. That has to be a big part of the day for any writer.

I think this is true even for writers who are thinking about important social issues like racism, misogyny, violence and economic exploitation in sophisticated ways. Claudia Rankine is not just talking about the often ignored prosody of her prose poetry when she writes that "a share of all remembering, a measure of all memory, is breath and to breathe you have to create a truce— // a truce with the patience of a stethoscope." René Char seems to have conducted his art by some imperturbable method even while fighting for the Resistance, and then, later, in postmodern France with its own noise. "The poison of the honey bee / Is the artist's jealousy," as William Blake says. In the end, the Baltimore laundry place at the center of the characters' lives in the John Waters movie *Pecker* is a lot more creative than the art gallery scene. Find that place for yourself, one way or another. It might have been a good year to throw away all smartphones, to disappear from all social media right from the start. But the imagination is adaptive, and I suspect that by the time I know that some poets have felt insulted, they have already turned insult into dare and completely launched poems of astonishing clarity.

People sometimes disparage the ideals of originality and authenticity as constructs that have bad effects. Back in 2004, I luckily got the chance to review *Phoebe 2002* for free, the compendium poem that retells the movie *All About Eve,* the classic and acerbic Bette Davis movie about a treacherous understudy who worms her way into the life of an initially unsuspecting actress. I love this giant and various book by David Trinidad, Jeffery Conway and Lynn Crosbie. The Phoebe theory of American poetry is that every kind of poetry has its originals, its Margot Channings and its immediate cunning Eves, and that the great majority of what we deal with when we look through journals and books is a vast wash of diluted Phoebe-dom, the imitators of the imitators, trying to find their own human way. This theory has a lot of appeal, aside from being a theory.

And, just as an aside, Sabrina, as for my behavior at that dinner party towards the end of last June, that was bad behavior of a totally different sort of horrible, but I was, in fact, really bugging you. I apologize. You know what William Butler Yeats says in "A Dialogue of Self and Soul":

> I am content to follow it to its source
> Every event in action or in thought;
> Measure the lot; forgive myself the lot!
> When such as I cast out remorse
> So great a sweetness flows into the breast
> We must laugh and we must sing.

> We are blest by everything,
> Everything we look upon is blest.

I can hear you putting this together the right way: "Guess that makes one of you, pretty grandiosely put for acting like a putz. You IS a putz, as Rimbaud puts it." Everyone is a Symbolist. Have to start somewhere.

Unpleasant people who can write well should not let their having crummy personalities go to their heads because good writers should be able to move from knowing their own inner workings to knowing some things about other people as well, and doing so with love. How well we do that is the actual worry and only originality. Have to start somewhere.

If Nobody Knows, That Is Fine

For poets who are conflicted about fending off/defending the institutional imagination, its discontents, while just trying to write living poems, a group that includes just about everybody, good or not in any way, part of the deal involves not knowing the quality of your own work and still trying to make it go. Things have changed and not changed, and our uncertainty has not changed at all, despite all of the marketing and self-marketing, and its attendant neurosis. Somehow, we have to make a friend of uncertainty, make it our useful goad, so that we don't act or think like various versions of small-town rubes. If I had to define the institutional imagination, I would say that it is what none of us entirely can escape any more than we would live without ethics or love, but which also hems us in with caution, vanity and convention. "I protect my good name," Milosz chides himself, "for language is my measure." Here are some current modes of the expected:

1. Subject is way more important than anything else, including language, seriously thesis-driven.
2. Character of speaker is posed as sage, as sensitivity, good information, vatic character, or nice. In any case, the character of the poet is static or flat, but good, so worth hearing.

3. Creates multiple book-length projects rather than collections of single poems with everything on the line, has either academic or marketing ethos.

4. Aesthetic safety first: poems that could survive scrutiny by a table full of graduate students with a wide range of similar aesthetics.

5. A lot of it is one big prose poem, a form that requires body as much as any other kind of poem, looks serious and easy at same time.

6. Preaches to choir rather than risking gray-area, subversive or satirical styles that could be misconstrued or resented for a cloven foot.

7. Everything is rhetorically touching. Spoken word meets university, seeks poet-audience hookup because it is always Thursday night here, people.

8. Poet can obviously spell the word *ekphrasis,* not *schmaltz.*

9. As for allusion (or citation), period-style forms of cultural allusion or subjects that do not result in body moving almost always suggest training.

10. The ultimate mode of the expected, the imitation, or the just plain corny is the humorless apocalyptic, but the absurd will make its comeback and help us survive.

Alice Notley claims that "only a voice can cut through" what she calls "the perpetual creation of convention." While anybody writing in the era of social media broadcasting and performance lectures can slide into marketing ethos and sanctimony, it may be more to the point to say that while a poem must have social intelligence, poetry needs weird subjectivity or risk to live, and all living poetry, whether esoteric or not, mediates these contradictory qualities. When we meet a poem that has a measure of sophistication but still rolls a flat tire despite the fact that maybe a lot of people think otherwise, we are on the trail of the unwritten rubrics of the institutional imagination, that which causes so much boring and well-intentioned writing, including much of my own. As Steve Almond says, the superego makes lousy art. This line of thinking, my own habitual bus route, and maybe yours, misses a number of big things, no doubt, such as some goodness of discovering like-mindedness in a world without community. My mother used to bring us to a food co-op in the basement of a progressive church. There were flies on the grapes and cheese. It was still life.

Even so, I began this essay just imagining that what happens when we read good poetry is like being on a street at night with various poets peacefully taking refuge behind garbage cans, or revealing themselves as gods or aliens, or aggressively preparing to throw down. But how far can such an image take us? Remember Merwin's great poem about Berryman.

> I had hardly begun to read
> I asked how can you ever be sure
> that what you write is really
> any good at all and he said you can't
>
> you can't you can never be sure
> you die without knowing
> whether anything you wrote was any good
> if you have to be sure don't write
> ("Berryman")

The wonderful thing is that whole business is just in our heads, as so many things truly are. One nice Sunday afternoon this summer, Sabrina and I crossed the train tracks that separate suddenly crunchy Somerville and now less crunchy Cambridge and went across town on foot. Somehow, we found ourselves wandering around the Longfellow Mansion, struck by the Teddy Roosevelt uniforms of the United States Park Rangers, the feeling of friendship and family, the good bad taste of the many landscape paintings—nothing there like a Mount Etna blasting a night sky to get Pompeii—and how Longfellow's last living daughter had had the old gaslight fixtures over everything inside rewired for electricity a few years after World War One.

Walking back home, I thought of how that apparently very gentle Henry Wadsworth Longfellow cat, just being there, in that little yellow mansion he may even have thought that he actually expanded by himself, and deserved, once drove Edgar Allan Poe crazy enough to commit book review. Who deserves anything? Let's be honest about our gifts and free.

My Boston School of Poetry

Early for Profit

One of the things about poets is that they pop up in the strangest and most unforeseen places. My Black Mountain was a little applied-arts school called Massachusetts Communications College. Later, it became the New England Institute of Art. A lot of what you hear about for-profit education is true. The schools can be awful and cynical, as can some supposedly non-profit schools that have horrible rates of student retention and graduation, and the whole system that has spawned such grotesque price tags on college tuition is at the very least a head-scratcher. And even though the good newspapers and public radio stations seem to be forever dragging out some graduate who can not find a job, and even though I would campaign for the top state attorney Maura Healey myself should she run for governor of Massachusetts, I have to say that I had a great time at this school.

And so did most of my students.

Like Black Mountain College, Mass Com, as we called it, featured hands-on learning. Unlike Black Mountain, it also inflicted the defensible style of outcomes-based assessment on its students, and, as I said, it was a for-profit school. It began as something called the Norm Prescott School of Broadcasting, and then it was the Northeast School of Broadcasting for a few decades on Marlborough Street in Boston, and then a couple of entrepreneurial guys named Howard and Peter bought it back when Clinton was president, renamed it, and then started hiring imaginative people to start degrees in web development and audio. They got it regionally accredited by its prestigious-sounding New England higher-education accrediting body and licensed by the Commonwealth of Massachusetts, and then started plastering the subways of Boston with its ads.

The ads were pretty good. One said,

Turn the volume up to do your homework—

And it showed a grungy kid wailing away on an electric guitar, hair in the air. They also had shirts that said,

Our school really sucks at football, but we have a hell of a band—

All of this was a little dubious. The place, after all, was not Rock and Roll Community College. I hear that somewhere in *Infinite Jest,* there are radio ads for Massachusetts Communications College. I am not sure if that is serendipity or not, or if Wallace also saw our ads and wondered, "What is that place? Probably nothing. I'll make something up about it."

I stumbled onto the place in the summer of 1997 through the want ads in the Sunday *Boston Globe* spread out on a table at the public library. I had moved up to Boston the previous fall from North Carolina after teaching in Greensboro for a year, and then spent the year frantically mailing out Xerox copies of my meager resume, with its four or five published poems and my one year of post-graduate teaching experience. I divided my time between waiting tables, working in the phone sales office of the Boston Ballet, and going to poetry readings several times a month in Cambridge. Although I wrote every day, I wrote badly, hermetically, and weirdly, trying to make sense of the new world of pain and disorientation that I found myself in as I headed into my later twenties. There are few things more depressing than being a graduate of a creative writing program and realizing that your adventures in the Vale of Soul-Making have just begun. Of course one is grateful for the experience anyway. Finally, in late spring, I landed an August interview for the expository composition program at Boston University, but it was a bittersweet victory because I was told that whether I got the job or not, it would be "maybe one class and maybe two," and there would be no chance of classes in the spring term, that institution being a front-loader of comp classes taught by non-graduate students. So I was not about to quit my nighttime job as a waiter, and I continued to moon over the Sunday want ads in the Medford Public Library. That's how I found out about Massachusetts Communications College. They had a nice-looking ad, away from the education listings, planted in the spreads for the tech start-ups.

They called me to come in for an interview maybe three days after I mailed in my application. It turned out that the new head of liberal arts there was a young poet, a year older than me, Jenny Miller. She was a fan of the poets I studied with in Greensboro, Alan Shapiro and Stuart Dischell, and she had actually been an editorial assistant for the journal that had published my third poem. "You're going to love it here, David. This place is going to grow. And we're going to hire ALL POETS to teach the English classes. Because poets are the only people who really understand punctuation, and these kids need poets because they all want to be rappers and rock stars. You will love it." It turned out that one of the owners of the school, Peter Miller, loved poets too. He had gone to Antioch with a bunch of writers and had majored in Chinese literature or something there. Hiring Jenny was a natural for him. He knew poets had heart and would be hungry. And so we were. And Jenny was true to her word too. She hired almost only poets to teach English, and even after she left, the people who took her place followed her, did the same thing. So even when we were bought by the then fast-growing Education Management Corporation, which turned us into the New England Institute of Art, they let us keep doing our thing, hiring poets and writing curriculum for a long time. Of course, now we're going out of business.

Ten years ago, I could take a walk around our offices, and the people I would run into were amazingly musically connected. There was the sharp-dressed and snazzy studio guy Don Puluse who worked on all of those great Columbia Records albums with Miles Davis and Bob Dylan and had run the audio program at Berkeley. There was Al Shapiro, who was there turning console nobs with the Stones and John and Yoko. There was Larry Miller, one of the inventors of free-form FM radio. Griel Marcus dedicates his book on the Doors to Larry. There was the disc jockey Gerry "The Duke of Madness" Goodwin. Gang of Four drummer Hugo Burnham designed the Freshman Seminar course. The place was crawling with legend past its moment. For many years, the head of career services was a dapper and hilarious Englishman named John Lay who had been one of the managers of the group Squeeze. It also had its own recording label, and the students worked with a faculty documentary film director, Tim Jackson, a well-known drummer in Boston, to produce several documentaries on things like culture jamming and the American Repertory Theater in Cambridge. The Czech performance artist Milan Kahout would just send a cassette tape and a rooster to our faculty readings. Nobody had a cassette player. Then when the school started offering a photography degree, that department hired all young artists. All these people were great, concerned teachers and, true to our broadcast roots, champion shit-talkers, believers in tough love, and survival skills. Music people, in particular, work together. Office hours were busy everywhere, as the faculty was available.

But for me, the best part was the poetry I got to hear. The place to be was not with famous poets. This was the place to be if you wanted to be with poets who were going to publish their first or second books. If we did an anthology of the faculty, it would be much better than any of those "Best Young" poets anthologies, which, like all anthologies and similar such pomps, are a product of the machinery of what Emerson or Thoreau calls the "courtier-like success" that has been the hallmark of American letters for as long as there has been an American literature. I'll take the poets I worked with—Joseph Lease, Camille Dungy, Tanya Larkin, Tom Yuill, Gregory Lawless, Sam Witt, Sam White, Dorothea Lasky and Jessica Bozek—buy all of their books on Amazon or from wherever—over any seemingly unified movement. And then there were the frequent visitors who used to drop by our classes and in for readings, David Ferry (young for ninety), and especially my friend Steve Almond dropping by workshops almost every semester for a few years and reading stories from his freaky books, and highly original Peter Richards there with *Oubliette, Nude Siren,* and *Helsinki,* some of the most original books of poetry around, and several times, David Rivard. Stephanie Burt was there for us too, and she and Rivard even came to say goodbye when we had a final alumni/faculty reading.

I am not really tempted to call these poets and writers a school like the Black Mountain School or the New York School, as they seem to stand for contrary and even contending impulses more than anything else, but they were my school and hearing their poems took my own poetry to school. If you just came upon their poems in journals or the books they were writing at the time, you might see them differently, maybe in terms of their lineages. Tom Yuill's *Medicine Show* could sound like southern narrative or elegiac formalism, but earthy. Joseph Lease would sound like what he is, somebody using unlikely, almost flat language musically, almost as if small Robert Creeley poems were blown up. Creeley liked him, too. Working on her first book *Awe,* Dorothea Lasky, if you had your ears cocked around Boston around 2004, she would sound like nobody else, comic and heroic. Dottie later also became an astrologer. And so on. The clannishness of aesthetics is a kind of miserable subject. God knows what I sound like, but hopefully I sound like somebody who listened to these poets develop, which is what I am. I am still trying to figure them out, and they are all continuing to make new things. How I love them, my old comrades from the for-profit art school world. You can grow some good stuff in a coal mine.

The question remains: why even want to call them a school? They are all so different. True, they *are* all so different, and I'm not even saying that they were all actually paying attention. Poets can be heavy hitters in terms of self-involvement, from the goofiest graduate student to the biggest star. But what these poets have in common is a sense of life. Go read some Tanya Larkin poems. Part of the reason she writes that way is that she has taught fifteen classes in a year, with real human beings depending on her to make things clear. I have seen other overworked labor forces who generate comedy and pathos this way. Hungry waiters. People who want to write poems often find ways to coddle themselves, but you can not really believe in coddling yourself if you have to work a lot. Their poems were not content to merely potter about the house sharpening pencils and eating cheese, reminiscing for no real reasons, sleeping in haylofts, narrating. At the dawn of the era of extreme and cautiously polished professionalism, when everything becomes a package, none of these poets cared to be further processed and mentored by the machinery more soul-flattening than the MFA machine, doctorate programs, creative dissertations and the like, most of them—like most graduate programs in general—dominated by hacks and grinds, and so chosen for professional reasons. The coming of age of dullness is age. Most any other ship would not have been much of a poet pirate ship.

Not really being institutionally mentored or excessively developed used to be the only common experience of poets. Once upon a time, geniuses like James Tate and Etheridge Knight could practically wander in off the street and set up shop. No graduate degrees for Heaney. Writing colonies and their like are some bad news. I have a brochure for one. This poet is holding a mug of tea with two hands. At ten a.m., she has a wedge of cheddar cheese and some walnuts, and then she goes back to her desk. It's so good that she has time to write. Another thing these poets have in common is the bottom-up sympathy that is the heartbeat and deep spring of the best poetry, period, and in its least feigned, non-nostalgic and unselfconscious forms always goes with an impatience with what can be called *ideational nattering*. If you lack a sense of timing, if you are too self-indulgent, you lose the audience that does not feel that they have to be there in the first place, that is, in fact, making an exception and big change by being in school.

A lover of pomps and intellectual machinery for their own sake could never teach our students—not that we all wouldn't have jumped ship for a more stable professional life—and the word-of-mouth would be so awful, or their bored students would sleep a dull blade out the door. In his great satirical book *Class: A Guide through the American Status System,* Paul Fussell makes the crack that the best way to bug a college professor is to call him or her "an educator."

But poets who wanted to mix it up with the kids dropping beats or blowing their eardrums out doing live sound at VFW hardcore shows, poets with shaggy-dog sympathies, and a sense of the beauty of the hodgepodge street, they could take the Orange Line and saunter over to Columbus Avenue to our place in the Pledge of Allegiance Building between the Back Bay and the South End, or roll on up on the slow boat Green Line train to Brookline Village (or as some kids would say, *the Illage*), this sort of poet would find not only love but inspiration. In other words, when we step away from the hams and memoirs, there is a strain in American poetry that is impatient with the processes and the patina of self-contained short or long lyric, which overtakes all of the various poetries, and then there is the real right thing, and for a while, it was here. This strain is called "the good stuff." Being *so brilliant* or *so sensitive*—expensive, enervating qualities—or wanting props for these qualities, whatever they are under the hood, where they belong—was out for these punky characters, the students and the faculty. An inspiring story costs a lot.

Yeah, I know, how unlikely. Kind of perfect too. Of course somebody's Black Mountain School is going to be a suckerfish on a for-profit in the age of Clinton and Bush. And of course, the shark would finally figure out a way to scrape the unsuspected art off while dying its ridiculous death. That is just the way creative things often are: temporary, unplanned, accidental, usually despite and not because of their supposedly sustaining institutions. The soul-making happens when nobody is looking, and nobody really ever is.

In 1997–1998, Jenny hired me, Joseph Lease, maybe three other poets, and some fiction writer. I think his name was Bud. She hired him because he looked a bit like George Clooney, we joked, and later, sickened by the adjunct life, and already sporting Clooney-style grey wisps, he got a real estate license. I once ran into him buying a bottle of wine about ten years later. He almost gave me his card. He was probably the last fiction writer who joined the faculty for over ten years until Steven Lee Beeber came on board, the author of *The Heebie-Jeebies at CBGB's: A Secret History of Jewish Punk.* I taught my first creative writing class there in the winter, in a television-studio classroom, where we would eventually have our first readings by visiting poets, and I also taught a developmental English and study skills class with about three students in it. That first year, I was also the head waiter at a restaurant, laughing my head off and sweating with line cooks and then figuring how much of a formalist I wanted to be with my head-bangers, most of whom, I can see now, were just a few years younger than I was. Getting some roommates, I was able to make do on my tips and adjunct money, as long as I lived in a dull neighborhood, Medford Square, the dullest—and impossible to give anybody directions on how to get there due to the whacked rotaries and intersections at the end of Mystic Avenue, the bumpy street that runs parallel to Interstate 93. People who live there don't want to be found. Might have gone back to school then.

In 1998, my second year at the school, the student body tripled in size, so Jenny hired more poets. Tom Yuill, who would eventually publish his first book with the University of Chicago Press and become a full-time faculty member and my best friend there. Jason Roush, a very good poet. Camille Dungy was there, too. She was a student in Greensboro the last year I was around that program. In the spring, the four of us and Joseph and Elizabeth read for the first time, in the cafeteria. Joseph would hold forth in the faculty lounge and explain about how banks red-lined African American neighborhoods and lecture us on the structure of institutional racism. That spring, he would get his first full-time teaching job and leave. Nice to know you, Joseph. Tom and I hung out with Jenny, Lynn, Camille and our Greensboro friend Steve Almond and sometimes read each other's poems, or went to readings, or we would get lunch, groups of us. Jenny had a place in the North End: rooftop parties at Jenny's. We could smell the salt air gas tanker harbor. How romantic.

The Motorcade

That spring, a few things happened. For one thing, Jenny found a new job, and we got a new department chair, which meant Elizabeth got promoted to take Jenny's course load and assist the new chair. Another thing that happened was Camille was hired away to her first full-time job at a school in Virginia. This allowed me to snake on in and claim her classes not only at Mass Com, but also to apply for and get her classes at Boston College. Thank you, Camille, for putting the word in for me in Chestnut Hill. I needed the scratch to buy a refrigerator and an engagement ring, and the kids never wrote run-ons. At Mass Com, my new department chair approached me sometime that summer and handed me a copy of the newly published *The Norton Anthology of African American Literature.* He was a social science guy, this department chair, so he was not all that smooth and human when it came to interactions, and though very liberal, he was also very wooden. "Well, David. I have a class for you. It's African American Lit. If I can find a black scholar, I will give it to him or her, but could you read up on this and be ready to go in September? That would be great."

I sort of hefted the book in my hands. That thing was heavy. I had been coveting it in the bookstores, but this was the first one I had gotten my hands on with the plastic wrapper off it. I thought it was funny that this guy was talking about finding some scholar of any kind. Like scholars were just floating down out of the trees—mostly white ones, but sometimes an African American one or two—and they were going to sign on for $1800 per class, the Social Security taxes not even taken out because maybe Howard and Peter figured the independent-contractor audio cats would prefer it that way. Indeed, they did. I felt that this place was the Wild West of education, funky and innovative, not lawless or anything, but coming into focus, improvisational. The kids were great—as a matter of fact, we were the kids, too—and the bosses were human, but there was not a whole lot of academic pomp to draw the scholars in, or enough bread, even for scholars. At our graduation, they played a hip-hop recording of "Pomp and Circumstance." The place was like heaven for young poets, but not for everybody.

"I'm not sure. There's a whole lot I don't know here. I wouldn't know where to begin."

"I'll tell you what. Think about it. Read around. The first day of class, you can ask the students if they want you to teach white American lit or do they want you to teach them African American lit."

"Let me think about that one, too."

The guy was a droid, like C-3PO. He didn't last long. We were wandering around a spaceship. One day I saw him in a broom closet, wires coming out of his belly, a mess. He moved on. He had his reasons. Businesses are tough. A lot of the hostility people feel towards higher education, and probably knowledge in general, is that they regard tenured faculty as lucky, not very energetic souls with sinecure positions that isolate them from the traumas and basic unfairness that other American workers experience as the normal flow of events. Well, I can understand that attitude. Do I take liberties? My memory is not all that accurate, except that it is.

That summer, I had but one lonesome class to teach, so I got my butt back into the Boston Ballet phone sales room for the annual fundraising campaign and got some lady to give the organization thirty grand on my first call when I spilled my coffee on my fundraising script and yelped in pain and told her all about it. I was in love, and my future wife Sabrina was living in New Britain, Connecticut. We conspired to be together almost constantly when I wasn't working, but midway through the summer, bread got tight, so I started doing some office temp work, but still managed to have a good time. I basically worked day and night four times a week, pulled an afternoon office shift, and got myself on the bus. The entire month of August, when my summer session class ended, I landed a month-long gig working as a replacement receptionist for the Commonwealth of Massachusetts Department of Veteran Affairs over by the North End, where I began to read *The Norton Anthology of African American Literature*, plowing through all the Dubois and the Hurston and Baldwin and John Edgar Wideman and enough Ellison and Wright that I knew I would love it. I figured that if the deal came down, I could handle myself and set up a good environment. Other things I read some of, and decided they sounded good, and I would put them on the syllabus. So there was Jean Toomer waiting for me. And a whole bunch of poets of the Black Arts Movement. And I would teach *Sula,* though I had never read it. One day, I brought the American Lit anthology with me. I knew I could swing that, having T.A.ed an American Lit class in Greensboro, but I didn't want to deal with that. I wanted the best. This was what I needed.

The class turned out to be just four kids. There was a scrawny white studio rat with ropy arms, and a massive, silent Cape Verdean kid from the working class town of Brockton or someplace like that, and a quiet and extremely awkward girl with ropy pigtails and an overbite. A few years later, her complicated secret life would have involved anime and online gaming. Maybe it already did. And then there was Dwayne. Except that he was on the short side and he had his hair slicked back and dyed the color of a canary, Dwayne walked just like the dancers at the Boston Ballet, which was down the block from school in the South End, where he was couch-surfing.

I had the two anthologies with me, and I held each one up. "Okay, you all signed up for African American literature, but my friend Camille Dungy—you know her?" None of them did. "She got a full-time job, so she moved to Virginia, and now I'm teaching this section. Now here's the deal. I've never taught African American literature. I read African American literature because I read the good stuff, but in the past, I have actually taught a general American literature class. If we make this an African American lit class, I will be learning right alongside you, and it might have to be a bit loose, like I'll give you a ton of a reading, and then we'll get to class, and we'll hash it out. We'll see what you read and what you think of it. And we'll go from there. Or I can give you a new syllabus next week."

The two silent kids kind of looked down and said nothing. "Man, I don't care one way or the other. I don't really want to take an English class," the Cape Verdean kid said.

"Fucking A, " the white kid said. "Let's do it."

"Do what?"

"African American literature. I am down."

53

Okay.

"What about you, Michelle?" I asked the young lady. I can't for the life of me remember what her name really was. *Dwayne,* I remember, because you remember genius that announced itself to you.

A whisper. "It's okay."

"It sounds experimental. It sounds like a good idea, all of us learning about this together," Dwayne said. "I took an African American literature class at Northeastern before I transferred."

"Dude, what are you doing *here?*" the white kid asked.

"Studying video. I want to work in film." He looked real sad, uncertain, worried, depressed, but also beyond a certain amount of things. "I'm relieved to have a class with some things to read in it."

"Okay, African American Literature it is." So I handed out the reading list. It went something like this:

Week One: Frederick Douglas and Phillis Wheatley
Week Two: W. E. Dubois, Paul Laurence Dunbar
Week Three: James Weldon Johnson and Zora Neale Hurston
Week Four: Countee Cullen and Langston Hughes
Week Five: Jean Toomer and Richard Wright
Week Six: Ralph Ellison and James Baldwin
Week Seven: MIDTERM WEEK and Robert Hayden
Week Eight: Gwendolyn Brooks and Lucille Clifton
Week Nine: Amiri Baraka, Ishmael Reed
Week Ten: August Wilson
Week Eleven: John Edgar Wideman
Week Twelve: Toni Morrison
Week Thirteen: Toni Morrison
Week Fourteen: FINAL EXAM

This was the only time I ever gave a class a syllabus without page numbers. "Just read it all. We'll figure out the good pages together" was my cheerful directive. The students had to keep a reading journal and the first half hour of the class was an in-class writing based on what they found in the reading, and then we would talk. Over the years, I would develop a lot of tools as a teacher that I didn't possess yet, like knowledge for instance. Today, I would not assign such an insane amount of reading, and I would use more small group activities even with a small group, and I would probably have the students do presentations. Today, I would also assign more poets. And maybe that's what I intended to do at the time, but the white kid went into rehab, and the Cape Verdean kid dropped out of school after the third week, and soon it was just me, Dwayne, Michelle, and the brilliant editorial and visionary hands of Nellie Y. McKay and Henry Louis Gates. But Dwayne arrived in class every week with five to ten pages of beautifully observed comments about the reading written in a neat and elegant hand. We spoke almost only of the literature. It was not the first class I would teach at the school that was half basic repair and addition of polish and half a graduate seminar in terms of insight and sweep. If you can teach well at a school with loose admission requirements and a curriculum that will also attract some great students, your business must be pragmatism and respect. I don't know how good I was.

I still remember the joy of discovery of all that fabulous writing: Zora Neale Hurston's essay on decorating with milk bottles—"Home-made, home-made"—all of those Baldwin essays, the hypnosis of Jean Toomer, the great range of Brooks, her gorgeous poems of the late 1960s based on the free space of conversation with her students, Ishmael Reed's boat of Ra and his Chattanooga poems, the first chapter of *Invisible Man,* all of it, all that mixture of tone and range and expressiveness, and the holy sentence, and Wideman's brother Robbie and August Wilson, Pittsburgh, Pittsburgh, Pittsburgh, and friendship in its osmosis and complexity, and Baraka, and *Sula.* All of this genius work reminded me to love language, capaciousness of poetry and prose. That anthology was against everything rotten in the world and made the country seem better. I also remember Dwayne thinking the prose of James Weldon Johnson was a big bore, Phyllis Wheatley "of historical interest, sorry," and Richard Wright, "kind of a dick." Dwayne knew Eldridge Cleaver was a homophobe. Who can or should agree with everybody? We should have read Etheridge Knight.

I never took or taught the class again. How could it ever be as good, my favorite class, and my favorite year? That fall, the school got bought by the company. They changed our name—first to the New England Institute of Art and Communications, and then to the New England Institute of Art. All of the adjuncts who were teaching three classes were promoted to full-time faculty members to teach fifteen classes per year. I was riding high then. I used the extra money from my classes at Boston College to buy a Sears refrigerator (having been able to afford only a dorm-sized bartender's fridge picked up used in Malden) and a vintage—cheap—engagement ring to bring Sabrina, the love of my life, to Massachusetts from Connecticut. The school grew to close to 2,000 students, and then we were sold again, and the markets crashed in 2008, and then things went downhill. Books were written by many. Poets came. Poets went. It was a lesson in American corporate procedures—the same boat as a lot of people in the world of cubicles and suits—and now we are closing our doors. We had the same number of students in the fall of 2015 as we did in the fall of 1997. I'm there a few months more, with a new book out, and another new book coming out in the fall, but I'm going to have to get a job, or a bunch of jobs. It's the way things go. All I have is a mortgage, two cats, two cars, a wife, a daughter, and heart. And experience. But let's not talk about my feet, how awful they are now. Let's build something, people. I'm not complaining. Sure, I felt like a professor sometimes, the way Doc Holliday was a doctor. I was a good gunslinger. It wasn't dentistry. I could teach a room. Any room. I have more good news to bring. Let's start another school. Get me some chairs. Get me some people.

The last night of the African American Literature class, I wandered up Berkeley Street towards Boylston from Columbus in a soft rainy mist. By December, I knew that my adjunct purgatory was coming to an end, and though I was tired from teaching all fall—after-apple-picking tired—I felt good. On either side of the street, the Boston

Police were setting up sawhorse-style wooden barriers. "What's happening?" I asked a cop.

"Clinton's motorcade is going to come through."

Wow, I thought. I love that guy. Just months earlier, he had finally beat the blow-job rap. I had heard the news on the radio while taking a shower, and I had whooped with delight, perhaps my happiest experience in non-sexual bathing, that sweet springlike day. How could anybody be a Republican after that? I had no idea what was in store for the nation. That same day, I was probably listening to news of some rehashed bombing in Africa. That was public radio for you. "Well, I'm just going to smoke a cigarette right here then and wait for him."

A few moments later, Dwayne wandered up, in his sad and elegant dancer's way, his hair blue and yellow now, his light raincoat tan as his razor-sharp sideburns. "What's up, David?"

"Clinton is coming by. I'm going to wait for him. The cops just told me."

He thought for a minute. "I'm going to wait for him, too."

A few minutes later, the motorcade came by. There was Clinton, happy to be back in Boston for the first time since his blow-job trials. Boston never let him down. Maybe Barney Frank was sitting there next to him, Barney, his strong defender. Barney has heart. I remember Clinton's blondish head in profile, like he was on a coin, William Jefferson Clinton. Give the man a nickel. Give me and Dwayne some jobs. We love you, Bill. Dwayne and I jumped up and down like pistons with our victory fists raised high in the air.

Poetics of *Mean Streets*, Again

Mean Streets is a hometown movie. I take myself out as I say that. Not my hometown. *Mean Streets* is like a guy frying sausages up, and then adding peppers and onions, and his daughter stands there watching him and smelling the good smell of a big, loving—well, kind of stormy, maybe—man cooking. I had a student from Northeast Philadelphia once. She liked that I immediately got the South Jersey references in her work. Her main need was to write about her father, who died when she was in high school. It's always good to have a Philadelphian in the room if you are around New Englanders. The Eagles are playing the Giants on a black and white countertop television. One of the antennae is made entirely of rolled tinfoil kinked twice around the tines of a large metal fork and balanced on top of the set.

Night falls on the hard-packed ice shaped by the ploughs. The Wild Card round ends. The family eats. The news comes on. Everybody walks away from the kitchen. If the television stayed on, there would be a nine o'clock movie. Then the eleven o'clock news. Maybe the Eagles won. Maybe the Giants won. There is a half-hour recap of the game. The reporter is standing in an empty locker room with underwear and jock straps all over the place. The reporter is wearing a lot of aftershave. Then in the world of old UHF and VHF television, *Mean Streets* comes on at midnight, a Sunday, midnight. There is nobody in the recliner, which is open as if somebody were in it. There is a lamp on. How do I know these things? I don't. I make shit up until things feel right. Cue the Ronnie Spector. "Be my, be my baby, / My one and only baby." I'm from Squirrel Hill, in Pittsburgh.

Mean Streets is the first art film I ever saw, even before *Baby, It's You,* that perfect movie. I could not believe its atmosphere of causeless, gathering momentum, and I am surprised I stayed with it. I stayed with *Save the Tiger*—"dull dull Dullsville"—because I liked *Some Like It Hot* and the Jack Lemmon parts of *Mr. Roberts.* Nothing seemed to be happening according to my own sense of pacing. I had seen seemingly all the Bogart and Cagney movies in circulation, the Marx Brothers. I knew that those old movies were fast-paced, and I knew movies could be great. I read all of the capsule reviews by Pauline Kael I could get my hands on. I read *Kiss Kiss Bang Bang* and *I Lost It at the Movies,* but I still thought maybe the Academy Awards meant something. To think otherwise was a sort of outrageous hypothesis. What? *A Passage to India,* no good. I didn't know what great was. Maybe Stanley Kramer. I sat through *The Color Purple* with my $1.75 box of Sno-Caps. Big prestige pictures were a lot more self-regarding than this one, even though it came off as some sort of autobiography. But this haunting movie was paying attention to its people, and they were all just sort of wandering around. Later on, I would watch—enjoy—other art movies about people just wandering around, *The Seventh Seal, Orpheus, The 400 Blows, Yojimbo, 8 1/2.* I knew, watching it, that watching *Mean Streets* had something more like the exposition to a book than a movie, and the characters were caring about important stuff, but after indicating caring and conflict, the movie just sort of let the people be.

I probably didn't notice the shot of the projector and certainly not as a sign of first-person moviemaking, but if I did notice this shot, I probably thought it looked like the grenade launchers the Corgi German army figures used to launch "potato-masher" grenades at the bright green American troops—so much closer to childhood. I didn't read the characters going to the movies a few times as anything more than what guys like that would do—like old teenagers. Now I see that they are going to an art house to see whatever was playing there, a Western, a Hammer horror film full of *Taxi Driver* blood. There is a poster for *Husbands* by John Cassavetes in the lobby when they buy popcorn to see a western, though the soundtrack is five or six years earlier. When he is unable to get that restaurant, when he no longer works for his Uncle Giovanni, probably Charlie will go to Fordham maybe, Good Pope John days, consider the priesthood, read Dostoyevksy and the Catholic existentialist Gabriel Marcel, who also believed that sacraments and grace only really happened on the streets, think Pope Paul is not so hot, with Church hang-ups about contraception or something. Who is that kid from Belmont, Don DeLillo? What's he reading, *Americana?* And here comes the worst Fordham student ever, that Little Lord Fauntleroy prick with the bizarre hair getting out of a cab, Donald Trump. He acts like his old man owns the Giants. Bighead Donnie—how did he get through the sophomore core class on epistemology? *You can't stand him* in the rain. He can go transfer to Penn, but Charlie will transfer to New York University, and become Martin Scorsese. He might not be a celibate, but he will be the President of Good Movies. It's a lot closer than taking the D Train to the Bronx. The implication of this and the idea of Charlie finding redemption in his own self-conscious way make this all pretty clear.

Later on, I would read "Ward Number Six" by Chekhov, while eating a calzone on Arthur Avenue in the Bronx. I remember thinking the calzone was heavy, that I had to pay attention to every single moment to keep on top of whatever insanity would happen next.

The movies, in general, are a good poetry teacher.

I think because we didn't have cable when I videotaped the movie, and the reception was so murky to begin with, I didn't get that the red lights of the bar are hellfire until I saw a clean copy of the movie. Soldier loses his mind and attacks the girl because he has been sitting with the loan shark, Michael. Michael has been buying him drinks and looking out with grim, malevolent disinterest, contemplating the betrayal of old friends, whether or not to cut them loose. I didn't see anything special about the blood. But maybe I didn't get this because I didn't yet have any vocabulary for the radiation of bad energy. The characters in *Mean Streets* radiate and believe in radiation of energy, and so does Scorsese. Charlie may not agree, but does not really think it is crazy that his uncle, the don, thinks that you should not sleep with epileptic girls because they are crazy. Crazy people you should avoid because they are crazy and not just because they ruin your reputation. On one level, *Mean Streets* may be about the social context of what passes for good judgment, but how confusing this is because we live in a world where everybody is throwing off a strong, palpable ambiance. The movie is religious the way that artwork in a church is religious.

Charlie believes that you have to wield some magic of personality. This is a movie about actors but not stars. Religion probably created magic and the actor at the same time. Sometimes the magic is good. Sometimes, it is bad. Happiness is committing to a role but is short-lived.

Mean Streets is a satisfying movie if you are a well-behaved person. It's about a conservative rebellion. Charlie breaks and does not break with any old codes, friendship, religion, family, love. When they come into conflict, he suffers throughout the whole movie. He acts and he suffers. He is like Sam Spade at the end of *The Maltese Falcon*— the first of the great noir non-code-breakers—only he is bleeding, his girlfriend is bleeding, his friend is holding his life in place by holding his hand to his wounded neck until the paramedics can get to him, and they are all going to have to make some sort of new accommodation with reality. Look how happy he looks in the front of the car driving away to Brooklyn. How decent and happy he feels right before the shooting, acting all heroic. He is planning to get them all to that motel cabin from *It Happened One Night*.

It is a deeply satisfying movie if you tend to be attracted to criminals and saints. When I saw this movie when I was fifteen, and again when I saw it on St. Marks in college as part of a double-bill with *Bang the Drum Slowly* just a few years later, I assumed the epileptic girlfriend was dying of her wounds, that Johnny Boy was dying. I got fooled by the little bit of silent movie closure that flashes in Charlie's head. He is making an interior movie, and they all die, except for him. His retreat and his fear involve a closure that the movie resists. If there is a closure, it is more like what happens at the end of "Everything That Rises Must Converge." When I see the movie now, I am impressed not just by the suffering of the characters or the sudden gore, but by their toughness. They will need that toughness because the sense of suffering at the end of the movie is exact, rational, and resisting the grandeur of closure. There might even be grace in the ending. All of this went over my head, and not like pigeons, but more like physics.

Jeff and I walked some produce across Murray Avenue to the kitchen at Rhoda's Delicatessen. There was an old African American guy rolling matzo balls into a big garbage can. I would fill in for Jeff at Engel's Fruit Market during the beginning of Passover. Sometimes, people from outside the neighborhood would assume I was Jewish. "Hey, man. Isn't today Rosh Hashanah? What are you doing here?" I considered this a big compliment. John Floyd heard the same thing. He was a Southern Baptist, but his father was a classics professor. The Floyds were from rural Virginia and Texas, and John's parents met at Oxford University, a couple of eccentric American Latinists. He was a carrot-top. White people look alike, some more so than others.

The Pope of Greenwich Village came out around that time, and by the time I saw that, we had cable television, so I taped it without fuzz or commercials. Daryl Hannah hopped around it in a leotard and wore lacy white underwear, saying, "Hey, you Irish asshole. I'm going to leave you for John John." Mickey Rourke had the best hair—like a straight Morrisey. I loved this stupid movie more than I could say. Not only this, it had an Irish American actor, a guy named Mickey, pretending to be Italian. It's basically *Mean Streets* without everything funky and seemingly plotless and with prettier actors standing in for the hyper realities of *Mean Streets*.

There were these two girls I bused tables with at Minutello's Italian Restaurant & Lounge. They were sisters and both track stars at Sacred Heart, the Catholic girl's school where really square girls went. The older sister was a knockout. She was legendary. The guys who ran track at my high school would talk about her, having only glimpsed her from afar. She was also a year older. The first couple of months I worked with her, I had a huge crush on her, and would basically stand around the bus-buckets with her, trying to think of witty things to say and of bits of physical comedy to make her laugh, which was tantalizingly easy. She was the reason my friend's boyfriend tried to get her to start lifting weights, to improve her pectoral muscles. Never forget how dumb teenagers can be.

Then her younger sister started working there. She had the same long straight nose. I like this kind of nose quite a lot. I would have been a bad plastic surgeon, always convincing people to keep their noses. Her sister was not as striking, but she wore her black work pants beautifully, and she had brown hair and eyes and the sort of long face that you do not notice as beautiful until you are totally in love with her face. This sister was hard to make laugh. She wore a kind of winter coat I don't see much anymore, but which is probably still strolling around Pittsburgh—a herringbone pattern, a large version of the pattern.

Once I ran into her and her father at the public library, and they gave me a ride home because I had a huge bag of books to check out for one of those twenty-page history papers honors students had to write every year in high school. When they dropped me off in front of my parents' big house, both their faces fell. They were helping a rich kid. Ewww.

Grave beauties.

If only they had been epileptics.

In *Mean Streets,* people cross the border of the invisible citadel and do not quite know that is the case, the heroin addict, the Jewish lady with her date, the stripper, the drunk gay guys. In Pittsburgh, neighborhood borders are geographic, all those Appalachian ravines depositing people. You don't just wander in. The city is not a continuum. It is a collection of villages. Nobody who just visits ever learns it. And families like mine—which came from New York or Chicago, university families—are forever only partially digested, except in Squirrel Hill or Shadyside, where we are happily collected as just some more cosmopolitan metal filings drawn to the big diaspora magnet of mentality. When Michael Chabon called his Squirrel Hill novel *The Mysteries of Pittsburgh,* some people said, "Yeah, right."

One summer, I came home and took a job in the neighborhood, and I asked the other busboy why he worked so far from home instead of closer, and he said, "People are cooler here, if you are an on the street. I don't worry about getting jumped. Jewish people around here are not jumping people. I can get off the bus, walk here, leave here, and then get on the bus, no problem."

"I went to school in East Hills. Aren't there places to work in Wilkinsburg?"

"No, not really."

After work, the older waiters still talking about their hometowns out away from the city, all happy to be someplace they can be gay, mostly, the city, away from the savage gay-bashing they met away from the city, out among the future Santorum voters.

"Why do I live in Pittsburgh? Here I can be with my lover in the parking lot of a McDonald's and not worry about the dumb guys from the football team beating me up."

This was news to me. My part of Pittsburgh, a paradise of not getting your ass kicked for being real.

Half the guys who worked in the kitchen were Vietnam vets in their forties, black guys and white guys. They would reminisce about deserted intersections where they used to rumble before they went off to the war. "I probably kicked your ass. Let's smoke ourselves a joint after work. Who are we? The breakdown crew. This here now is neutral ground now."

For a movie filmed in Manhattan thirty years ago, *The Pope of Greenwich Village* has fewer black characters in it than *Alice* by Woody Allen, which does contain a variation on the single black sperm joke in *Everything You Ever Wanted to Know About Sex But Were Afraid to Ask.*

With its single African American stripper, *Mean Streets* shows something about the awkwardness about race found in people who live in enclaves that has the undeniable realism of truth: that longing and projection are as linked as shadow and sunlight. Charlie gets this about himself without heroic self-regard.

That the same insight was joined to madness and violence in *Taxi Driver* also worked on me in a similar but more awful way.

In *Mean Streets* and other Scorsese movies, human beings are irreducible to bromide, to *Places in the Heart,* with Sally Field, sexy blind John Malkovich, and saintly Danny Glover. Bromide loves closure.

The stripper is shown at the end of the movie in the montage of its major peripheral characters, tired and sitting at a table among the other characters not particularly moved or affected by Charlie's dilemma, all of them alone, together only as we see them. He is thinking of a movie and bleeding. They are not at all interested in being reduced to being characters in his movie, symbols, tokens, or anything like that at all.

Some people are doctors born who combine artistic and scientific intelligence. My friend Lou told me this story once, maybe in eleventh grade. He and one of our classmates whom we loved and warily respected because she was more advanced than us and, mentally, a tough cookie—later a novelist, a working writer—were walking down Shady Avenue. Lou is an otolaryngologist now. His brother Aaron, who is an ophthalmologist now, says that you have to be really good to be an otolaryngologist.

"What's your favorite method of masturbation, Lou?"

"My hand. Kind of a pump action. I find that very reliable."

"I like appliances." Take that, class clown, tight-ass, future surgeon. Whoever is really edgy is not you.

Leaving the restaurant, Ralphie says, "Hope you get some meat for that dog of yours."

Leaving the grocery store, Milt says, "If you are ever with a girl, make sure to wear a thingamajig on your schmeckel."

There is nothing that stupid in *Mean Streets,* including the fight with the pool cues.

Speaking of Joyce, as we just happened to be, *Mean Streets* is one of those what-would-have-happened-to-me-if-I-never-left / I-am-never-ever-leaving-here things. *Dubliners* is a hometown book. You feel gratitude for the great books you read when you were a kid. You feel even more gratitude for the great movies, for any utterly embodied and risked point of view—that world war artillery cannon projector Scorsese pointed at the camera, at the people.

Scorsese shows the theater-making impulse, and he loves it, but it is sad, wavering, contained, and potentially dangerous, a part of human nature, and never quite in synch with the world as events and other people happen.

The theatrical impulse in people is a hopeful impulse, as when the old waitresses at Minutello's disappeared at the end of their shifts into the bathroom and then re-emerged in plunge-line dresses carrying sequined clutch bags, trooping off in their hard-drinking old-lady waitress posse, their hair suddenly large and Egyptian or Roman, to Dells Lounge in Bloomfield, to get loaded and hear their Bobby Vinton songs there. There was Eve and Louise (with huge Broomhilda wig, singing about screwing her husband while sawing the bread for the bread box) and Erna, a German immigrant, pretty testy, and a hunchbacked waitress who made babies cry when she set up their high chairs, and Dottie, and so on. There was the manager El Sid, and the assistant manager, Ralphie, and there was his wife, Dodo, a former dancer of some sort who made the schedule and actually ran things on the floor, the maître d', the seater of parties, the closer of time, a small-g god.

Down on Murray Avenue, ten hours earlier, in the world of daylight and slow hours, at Engel's Fruit Market, the old man Milt and his daughter Claire were kind of sniffing at the air, wondering if Sam the punchy boxer chewing a spitty cigar he never lit, a little bit at a time all day, had lit an egg. Milt was generous. He got beaten up down South during World War Two, a draftee mouthing off to racists on a bus. He rode a freight train to Florida during the Depression, and it was so warm when he got there, he slept on a bench. Most of the customers were old people buying two or three things for dinner—a few cucumbers, a tomato, apricots, some iceberg lettuce. He would fall asleep across the street eating toast at

Rhoda's Delicatessen. We felt lucky to know him. He was the guard of something.

I would help Jeff move crates of oranges from the sidewalk in and to replenish the displays of apples and pears swaddled in their diapers of purple tissue. He teaches third-graders now at a Jewish day school in Marin County. My friend has the toilet-seat kind of bald spot going now. Just as we always suspected, he's turning into Milt. In a way, I'm turning into Sam. So many Pittsburgh kids end up putting sunblock on their bald spots in California or Florida. A childhood in Pittsburgh has a lifetime of clouds. What was Murray Avenue? An existential art movie, people wandering around, poking around, kids, senior citizens, a precipitous hill turning its citizens into classical goats, used books, used records, pizza, crummy winter, endless, going to the University of Pittsburgh, dull, entertaining, the capital of nowhere but commanding the closest scrutiny, the neighborhood, our own. Once, Milt found a dead tarantula in a box of bananas. "Be careful, you two, there might be a tarantula in there. You never know." I remember there was snow falling downhill out the big plate glass windows showing the downward tilt of the steep street.

Katie Peterson's Robert Lowell, Other People's Lowell, and the Existential Addressee

Robert Lowell. New and Selected Poems. Edited by Katie Peterson. Farrar, Strauss and Giroux. 2017

Robert Lowell is a poet who reveals our own idiosyncrasies as readers whether we read him or not. Good riddance to poetry fame and domination, but keep Lowell anyway. As Katie Peterson makes clear in her new selection of Lowell, which is a beautiful and idiosyncratic edition with a superb introduction, he is a poet of immense range and subtlety, a poet whose poems are "memorable for their language, not simply the vanishing facts of story" and who "remained constitutionally immune to any stultifying permanence either of form or of spirit." In other words, he is a model of development and change, almost in some Buddhist way, in his work. In her introduction, Peterson claims that he was not really to her taste, or at least a baffling presence, when she started studying him in graduate school as a Californian from a more rootless world of Beat poetry and drum circles, and that westerners have always found it hard to enter into Lowell's work.

I've heard different versions of this over the years.

One writer told me, "When I got out of graduate school, Lowell had just died. And so many people were either for Lowell or for Bishop. I decided to ignore them both and write novels." And that's what he did, about one per decade, as novel writing takes time.

Some of the Lowell partisans have always been kind of hard to take for social reasons, I am guessing. Years ago, I remember being at a party with a lot of grungy kids, and then my friend Dave showed up wearing his slacks and a tucked-in Polo shirt. He was drinking beer with one hand and holding his golfing gloves with the other. He was telling everybody to read *Notebooks*. This did not win Lowell any admirers. What can you say when somebody has grass stains on his white glove? Hand him a Becks.

Not so many years later, I was at a dinner with an anti-realist, hilarious, capricious poet who was always getting into scrapes with people, and who had strong opinions. Somehow, the poem "For the Union Dead" came up, and he put both his hands over his ears and shook his head violently "No no no no no no." The truth is he was from a social world of writers where *not even knowing Lowell* had cachet. He had a long no-fly list. The new twitched in some high grasses, and he was not going to be the rabbit in these particular grasses. Or perhaps one way of avoiding sounding like poets whom one finds turning up spent soil is to ignore their influences. Some people, you could never even get to read the beginning of "Waking Early Sunday Morning":

> O to break loose, like a chinook
> salmon jumping and falling back,
> nosing up to the impossible
> stone and bone-crushing waterfall——
> raw-jawed, weak-fleshed there, stopped by ten
> steps of the roaring ladder, and then
> to clear the top of the last try,
> alive enough to spawn and die.
>
> Stop, back off. The salmon breaks
> water, and now my body wakes
> to feel the unpolluted joy
> and criminal leisure of a boy—
> no rainbow smashing a dry fly
> in the white run as free as I,
> here squatting like a dragon on
> time's hoard before the day's begun!

It's a shame because Lowell at his best is a counterintuitive antidote against some self-involved mythologies.

Poems like "To Think of the Woe That Is Marriage" and "Waking in the Blue" are ones in which the speaker resists the cramped, unhappy spaces of acting nuts. The famous Lowell poems—"The Quaker Graveyard at Nantucket," "Skunk Hour," "For the Union Dead"—are justly famous even if considered purely on the level of sound and repay reading aloud and rereading for years, but they are also poems of capacious humanity and sharp-eyed social reporting that go further towards explaining the cross-currents and tensions of our culture than most poets could ever manage. Another great thing about Lowell, though a lesser great thing, is that he writes poems that are as multi-tracked in terms of meaning as French Symbolist poems. One of my favorites in this mode is "The Old Flame" from *For the Union Dead,* a poem that does not make the cut in Peterson's selection, perhaps because the marital ground is covered in other poems. In "The Old Flame," a couple who cannot get along are representative of an entire culture full of emblems and also entirely specific as Lowell remembers conversations in the bedroom of a former Maine house surrounded by cultural bric-a-brac. The wintry ending of the poem is worth thinking about:

> Poor ghost, old love, speak
> with your old voice
> of flaming insight
> that kept us awake all night.
> In one bed and apart,
>
> we heard the plow
> groaning up hill—
> a red light, then a blue,
> as it tossed off the snow
> to the side of the road.

These two are living the flag, old glory, an almost every-couple fueled by deliveries from the package store courtesy of a cab driver who is also the town sheriff. And what an invocation of intimacy, of her "flaming insight," which is still also compulsive, keeping them awake, as is the word *groaning.* That registers irritable pain and also compassion. These two are intellectuals. Truly after Ginsberg, in so many of Lowell's poems the ignobility and the nobility of the mind freely coexist, another marriage inside the marriage. Lowell's tough-minded humor is pervasive, though hardly foregrounded. He has a lot to tell us about how to live in these mishaps, about the double dilemmas we feel, registering the claims of one self against the claims of another, of strengths that are at times weaknesses, loves that are also irritants, and so on. It is a perfectly multi-tracked and humane poem, equal to human complexity, which can never be resolved except in the temporary endings of poems.

Once we get past the historical impulses in *Notebooks* and some of his other sixties poems and some dull stuff after "The Quaker Graveyard," Lowell is one of the most relational poets in the language, and even his historical and political pieces are animated by a sense of the primacy of personal intimacy, as when Lowell, with comedy and anguish, reaches out to the figures on the television at the end of "For the Union Dead" with no illusion that they reach out to him. Then come the sonnets, where a lot of people stop. There are so many of those sonnets, I don't think many people should read all of them, and certainly not all at once, but they are great to dip into to find amazing poems like his sonnet about Harpo Marx and the range of poems about other poets, especially the old ones. A lot could be said about Lowell as a prose stylist who brings the expressiveness of nineteenth-century prose into mid-century verse in his sonnets, but this style can grow adjective heavy with a moribund flavor of decay in a sequence like "Long Summer." Reading the sonnets, with their personal poems, historical poems, poems of moral combat with illness, and political poems, I feel that Lowell covers this ground more dynamically in *Life Studies* and *For the Union Dead*, books that stand up to decades of rereading as few books of American poetry ever have. Nevertheless, with their strong sense of occasion and range, the sonnets are another resource. Major Jackson builds on them in *Holding Company*. David Wojahn's memorable *Mystery Train* is practically a pastiche of the more public-spirited of them. Other people are more complex and more completely alive to him than other people are to most other poets in their poems, and this is particularly true in the sonnets as well.

A lot of people have noticed (Ian Hamilton, for instance) that Lowell embraces free verse after coming into contact with Ginsberg's first book, but Lowell's explicit embrace of even embarrassing parts of his personal life as a source in *Life Studies* and in all of his subsequent work is directly related to Ginsberg's great early books. I can think of only two poets with naked Lyndon Johnson poems. The other is Dylan. But I think that the thing about Lowell being personal is that he writes to people recognizing their complexity, and he never creates the impression that he just writes about them without calling into question his own detachment. Lowell is a poet of generosity and love. My favorite anecdote about Lowell is that around the time he was working on various books of sonnets, he ran into a recent college graduate, aspiring writer and Marine Corps enlistee from Providence by chance at a brunch. Lowell told him he should not go, and on Okinawa, the Marine became a conscientious objector. Between Lowell and reading Saul Bellow's *Herzog* from a camp library, the enlistee may not have had a choice. That young guy became the poet Fred Marchant. Thank God, and thank Lowell, and thank Bellow.

The way Marchant remembers the incident in his essay "Table and Doorway" suggests that the form of direct address and engagement that Lowell practices in his poetry was what he strove for in his life.

> "*And what about the Green Berets throwing the Viet Cong out of helicopters?*" ... I was a second lieutenant in the Marine Corps, an infantry officer on his way to the northernmost units in what was then South Vietnam.... Bloody Marys were going round.... My first response was to say I didn't know anything about those so-called "airborne interrogations." ... Lowell was having none of it. I remember even less of what he said in the moments that followed, but have an unequivocal sense of the angry, suspicious, and accusatory tone with which he said it. The tone said to me and everyone around us that I was no different from the ones who had tossed those guys to their deaths.... The table of about a dozen folks fell totally silent as he practically and loudly demanded that I

explain what was going on with this kind of behavior, and I imagine myself blushing, stumbling around for a word or two, but in the end saying nothing.

And then, despite the element of cruelty, there is something amazingly touching, eloquent, personal, and mysterious, even apologetic for the distances of his public consciousness:

> Edwin [the host of the brunch] walked me to the front door. I could see behind Edwin as he hugged me goodbye, that Lowell was racing to the door to catch up with us. He took my hand and looked me as directly in the eye as anyone ever has in my life and gave me the rhyming order to "Come back, young man, come back intact."

I feel that individually focused side of Lowell animates his poetry more than something abstractly idealistic.

In his Personism manifesto, O'Hara says that we should write poems to real people, not to other poems, and that leads to poems like "Personal Poem" and "Joe's Jacket," a poem of a relationship cooling off so embracing of nuance in its telling, it raises similar questions as the poems in *Dolphin* and the beautiful "Summer" sequence to Lizzie and Harriet: *How are you really here?* The great force of how reality is summoned, if not solved, by relationships and their conflicts and confluences, reconcilable or not, was in the existential water that people were drinking at the time, Buber, Sartre, Baldwin, and Camus all dealing with loneliness, engagement, relationship. After World War Two, traditional apostrophe becomes something else, something more than gestural. I think you can say that it becomes double portraiture and acknowledgment. The person-to-person turn comes out in poetry first, and then it changes popular culture through music. What this is founded on is still a good idea if we can find a language for it. In "Skunk Hour," the song on the radio "love, oh careless love" is an old blues.

Why You Never Run into Cosmo Topper Anymore— Reflections on Poets and Institutional Thinking

People talk about working on their brands. What is it about *Topper?* You never run into *Topper* anymore. It's one of the great Cary Grant movies that invented Cary Grant. There Grant is, sometimes stolid, sometimes irresponsible, with a surprisingly bitter streak for somebody so antic. Everything that is so relevant about the movie to imaginative life occurs in the exposition. When we first see live George Kirby, he is driving his convertible—a 1936 Buick tricked out with a single Buck Rogers spaceship fin on the back—drunk out of his mind, seeming steady, with his feet, his nice shoes. He and his wife Marion, played by Constance Bennett—her voice is full of money—are leaving a party at their house in the country and heading for New York sixteen hours early for a bank board of directors meeting, giving them time to stay out all night drinking in Manhattan along the way.

All through the bank meeting, George misbehaves and can hardly sit still. Grant plays this character the way he is written: a top-out-of-sight rich guy with ADD who feels kind of pissed off about it. He has snarling hatred for the also ridiculously rich but older man, Cosmo Topper. And Topper is not too crazy about George either. He has to tread carefully around George because George is a much larger shareholder than anybody else. George could depose Topper if he ever got too interested in the proceedings. We see Topper taking a shower, voluptuously enjoying it nude from the waist up, having himself an old-man ball, and getting ready reluctantly for work and bullied by his valet, who insists that he get to work on time. Topper doesn't really have to do the job, but he is doing the job, and we also get to see Topper's wife, played by Billie Burke—Glinda the Good Witch, Florence Ziegfeld's widow, so she was probably born in a trunk—but here somebody who truly cares about keeping everything proper.

The exposition of the movie also lets us know that Topper is deeply rattled by and attracted to George's wife, Marion, a charmer played by a charmer who flirts generously with the old man the way one might stroke a old, dusty, but extremely appreciative housecat's knotty, un-licked belly. When George and Marion get killed in a car accident on the way home, the couple discovers that they are not going anywhere because they have not done anything for anybody, which is not equally true of both of them. You believe that George is a restless, highly motivated ghost because Grant plays the inexplicable anger at Topper in the live scenes so precisely. In order to progress to the next life, George and Marion decide they have to help Cosmo Topper have a better time. Marion continues to treat Topper more or less the same way as she did while living. More laughs and sight gags ensue.

I never saw any of the *Topper* sequels or the television show, and I am glad because Cary Grant is not in any of them, though maybe I shouldn't be glad about missing more silvery Constance Bennett. While the *Thin Man* sequels burnish the original by being pretty good—even the bad ones—*Topper* has a post-Topper life that obscures it, and the only way to watch it now on my computer is to watch a fuzzy ghost of it on YouTube, unless I preferred to pay for some sort of bootleg DVD. *The Thin Man* is a joy because the movie puts two people at the center who do not need to develop. They are adults, and do not need to change, a completely faulty but winning idea of adulthood. Powell and Loy are lyric states, as Powell and Lombard are in *My Man Godfrey*, or Grant and Roz Russell in *His Girl Friday*, comedy of work done for love. The poet Peter Richards once told me that according to some barely understood cosmic law, a bad book of poetry can diminish the quality of an earlier, previously brilliant book of poetry by the same author, a theory which despite its only tenuous relationship to observable science has the ring of truth because it is that scary. The world should not work that way, but maybe it does. In any case, the print we get of *Topper* is snow city, perhaps from drifting in and out of public domain.

The greatest movie of this time period is *Bringing Up Baby*, the only Oscar Wilde movie ever made. Probably the reason it was a dud at the box office was its close embrace of pop-Freudian subtext repression gags as the expression of evangelical horniness—enduringly stylized, always anomalous, the scatterbrained tuxedoed paleontologist Cary Grant leaving a club and doing whatever that is with equally impulsive Katherine Hepburn through the geometrically gaping drapery of her damaged gold lamé dress. But it is similar to *Topper* in treating the rages of privilege as disorders of the seekers and keepers of class.

Acting these rages out, suffering them, is the main function of the character actor Eugene Pallette, the extremely fat actor with a loud voice roughened by tobacco and Tabasco sauce, touchy, easily pissed off in almost every funny movie made in Hollywood between 1935 and 1943—there he is as Friar Tuck brawling in a steel hat with Errol Flynn in *The Adventures of Robin Hood* over a joint of mutton in the middle of a river. Usually, he is a grouchy rich guy, rhythmically banging a silver butter dish for service in *The Lady Eve*, rolling his eyes and manhandling the gigolo in *My Man Godfrey*, a rancher in a tuxedo in *Heaven Can Wait*. He is a type, the rough millionaire Dan Cody from *The Great Gatsby*, the silver miner who built a mansion in Newport and died on the pot there. But in these movies he also a marker of what could happen to the leading man unless he gets his act together. He might end up unhealthy. He might end up eating Eugene Pallete. Eugene Pallette has eaten libidinous Eugene Pallette, performing a double function for the audience, for whom he functions as a bad-tempered, popcorn eating and still hungry stand-in for their own alienated selves, but also as a target for their universal, righteous, superior scorn. Of course, Eugene Pallette got the turkey leg.

We can say that there are two political parties of screwball comedies. The ones that include Pallette are decidedly liberal. His figure crowds out any rich and sensible father figures to emerge, dispensing stern-sounding council and correction. The real divides in this world are always between the metaphoric and the literal-minded. These unruly movies provide us both ways of thinking simultaneously. *The Philadelphia Story* turns on its bummer of a wise father speech at the end. Why listen to that guy? Naturally, Pallette shows up in *Topper.*

Garbage-truck Eugene, I like to think of him. He is often the only person in any of these movies who is not a police officer or a brassy maid who does not have a transatlantic accent evading precise location. Cary Grant was British, but so was Bob Hope. Preston Sturges knows the territory when he has Barbara Stanwyck feign a British accent in *The Lady Eve.* She pretends to think *Connecticut* is pronounced *Connect-It-Cut.* If you watch screwball comedies, that state and the Riverdale section of the Bronx are crawling with people with fleeting and impossible-to-place upper-class accents, part of the whole literature of British charlatans from *Huck Finn* to *The Hateful Eight.* But in these screwball comedies, possible British-ness goes along with the image of wealth directly or indirectly on display as a false image, a pale ghost of privilege, blondes. Maybe if you dig back far enough, you might find a couple of authentically imagined rich guys of the era. Maybe Warren William and Guy Kibee in *Gold Diggers of 1933,* their accents like Robert Frost buzz saws, pushing aside their bland green beans and coming down to New York from Boston to attempt to tag a couple of chorines, with the older of the two getting taken by the gay gold digger and Joan Blondell refusing to be had by the somewhat younger man. The old code no longer works, of course. Pallette is the Secretary of Hunger now, and Kibbee is Secretary of Bald, and Warren William is Secretary of Commerce. They all go around saying, "I started out as a humble blacksmith."

The great Sturges comedies from the early '40s have a pre-Code, New Deal mind. An odyssey with a side trip into melodrama, *Sullivan's Travels* is the only screwball comedy to address race, and it even messes with its own use of racist stereotypes in the "Uncle Ben in the

Airstream Kitchen" early sequences by bookending the movie with an entirely different representation of black people in a scene set in a church. The sanctimoniousness, falseness, and unconscious racial stereotyping of this well-meaning scene might embarrass or even hurt us more than the scene of overt racism it seeks to correct—Sturges has not been able to avail himself of Baldwin's "Everybody's Protest Novel"—Chuck Yeager sound there—but at least Sullivan learns that he doesn't know anything except comedy. The movie is not as sanctimonious or self-regarding as any of us can be when we really get serious and righteous, maybe not the best postures for any good fight for our lives. Screwball can be the antidote; screwball turns out also to be the diagnosis. Let's really remember Franklin Roosevelt like my grandmother.

Cosmo Topper ends up haunted by George and Marion when he starts driving their refurbished car, and thus continues to flirt with Marion, which ends up saving him. Aren't George and Marion and Topper really Mr. Bones, chicken paprika, and Huffy Henry? There is something perverse in Topper continuing to love what is dead in himself. Aren't all of these movies set in Wellesley, Massachusetts, or in Fairfield County, Connecticut? Aren't all of these screwball characters the nieces and nephews of Nautilus Island's eccentric millionaire or Eugene Pallette? Discovering the real England is a disaster for Plath, the place where her cut thumb has joined the Klan. The first time Tracy Lord and C. K. Dexter Haven are married, they have Robert Lowell's violent first marriage. Isn't James Merrill in fact the Merrill-Lynch heir, James Merrill? Let's see. What other world is as obsessed with lineage, pedigree, awards? Maybe, but only overtly, *Best in Show* comes close. Trophy culture is bribe culture. I blush for people who care about awards.

Perhaps we should all be thinking about *Caddyshack* in this one particular way. Who gets closer to Trump? Who gets to win? Between Dangerfield or Ted Knight, I will go with Ted Knight. Fluff that hair up. Dye him tangerine. Poetry can survive it all because "it survives / In the valley of its making where executives / Would never want to tamper," as W. H. Auden says, in those lines that explain what he means when he says, "poetry makes nothing happen." He did not mean that we should not have engaged poems like "In Memory of Sigmund Freud" or "September 1, 1939" or "Spain 1937" that form the constellation at the end of the book where "In Memory of W. B. Yeats" originally appeared. He was contrasting the freakish unlikeliness of poetry with the marketing mind, the logic of mass culture. For Yeats to become his admirers is a hard fate. Let's have a bloody good cry. Maybe a panel discussion would help.

Poets know that teaching is a privilege, and that's why they are not making sick money, except maybe some people. The effects of fully internalized and executed, institutional expectations on the imagination, even on poets who are not literally physically haunting the corridors of institutions, but who conceptualize their work and aspirations and annoyances with their received tools and expected pieties and postures, is a somewhat different issue than what imaginative people can do for institutional life, which is to improve it by being weirdly courageous. We need the unexpected imagination more than ever now that the world is so full of disaster and sources of outrage. What is *The Scarlet Pimpernel* about except that there should be no difference between here and there? It has the greatest poem ever done in a movie:

> *They seek him here,*
> *They seek him there.*
> *The Frenchies seek him everywhere.*
> *Is he in Heaven? Is he in Hell?*
> *That damned elusive Pimpernel.*

That's a British movie, wonderful, bonkers. Maybe Leslie Howard was saving the rich, but I still like the poem, which nutshells practically everything there is market-proof to say about the freedom and engagement of poetry under these conditions. And that poem is so good that the Kinks went and made "Dedicated Follower of Fashion." You know who does good work? Dentists. Everybody needs a dentist. As a matter of fact, I like poems in general, a lot—and poets, too, love lots of them. Poems are their own best descriptions and can have torn screens and enough holes in their ceilings to let the sun and the rain in and the hot air out. The rest of the machinery can never catch up. Can never catch up to *Easy Money* with Rodney Dangerfield.

In *The Other Voice,* John Ashbery comes up with a whole raft of motley, spotty poets who are his select group of poets that get him going when he needs help getting going, so I am not insisting on any categories that would lend themselves to a panel discussion. And come to think of it, if I check in with other poets, they are apt to tell me that they are out there mooning for some obscure things they know about. Here is the secret theme song of making poetry in general, courtesy of Groucho Marx, Bert Kalmar, Harry Ruby, and *Horse Feathers:* "I don't care what you have to say / It doesn't matter anyway. / Whatever it is, I'm against it...." The high-kicking shall make you free, if nothing else, actually a whole lot less. Not a job for a klutz. It's sort of like Robert Frost's "closed to all but me" line, or Lorca's "I'm not to blame" in his lecture about the poems in *Poet in New York.* Never encourage anybody to attend panel discussions at a writer's convention either. Encourage people to watch *The Apartment* and *The Fortune Cookie,* or, as it was called in England, *Meet Whiplash Willie,* instead. A little more Billy Wilder is always helpful, poetry-wise and ethics-wise, to echo his villainous office predators, with his movies made "for people with a sharp, aggressive attitude to life." The quotation is from Raymond Chandler's "The Simple Art of Murder." He was talking about Dashiell Hammett's first novels, but this seems like an admirable way to think of an actual audience, a dream audience or a dreaming audience, for the great American comedies, for instance, and the saving best and most concise lyric poetry that presents the range of recognizable human responsiveness in the resources and sensibilities of a voice.

All these poetry ghosts, where are they? No matter what they are talking about or how they are talking about things, it sounds like they are working at some college someplace and trying to think their way out of college. Talk about paradoxical. I read some of them every year according to my needs and lights, a bit here, a bit there, and they are getting clearer and clearer to me, more permanent, even as they fade away, screwballs, showing up, drinking bottled water or coffee, pottering around and writing about that, worrying, fretting at the office, politic, testing the winds, resentful, delighted, dutiful, maybe even a bit boorish—is that lamb korma on my lapel?—winning, losing, taking their stands, composing lectures on craft, getting pissed, preening, thinking they are so badass or miserable, doing their things, providing, as everybody must. Why do you never run into Cosmo Topper anymore? You just might be Cosmo Topper. Didn't you know? It was news to me, like a minty and lime-green lollipop, Topper.

Strange Digs and Jim Clark

for Victor Cruz

For somebody who has spent so much time alone in his life, I have not lived alone that much. Having the right kind of roommate is almost as good as living alone, especially if you have different hours and would never think of cooking a meal together because you just throw your face down into the trough. Coming from a largish family, and parents who were cramped in apartments as kids, I subscribe to a theory of family life that allows for personal space, something I think is part of my problem, the basic problem of life being selfishness. But the years I lived together with myself I consider good years, so I will always love where I lived on Walker Avenue, in Greensboro, North Carolina, trying to cook myself some black bean soup and filling the whole place up with bean smoke after soaking them so long and thinking they were pretty. Eating American cheese sandwiches on the cheapest white bread toast I could find with mayonnaise and horseradish. At times, it felt like being in some Beatrix Potter book with people, completely out of my normal experience, yet burrowed down deeply in it.

I found the place after looking for an apartment for six hours. My philosophy major friend, also named Dave, drove me down from Pittsburgh via side trips to Virginia Beach, where we went to a bar that shared a dance floor with an arcade that was filled with smoke, bad synthesizer music, enlisted men and women from the navy, and thirteen-year-olds who shyly tiptoed out of their gate still holding wooden ski balls and then tiptoed back to roll for more tickets, and Raleigh, where we detected faint smells of Republican in bars near our hotel. Neither one of us had consciously ever seen a crepe myrtle.

83

We thought the trees looked like pink, white and purple poodles, which they did.

I didn't know too much about Dave. He was from Pittsburgh, too. He had a single mom and was from the suburbs, and he loved the neo-Thomists. He wanted to go get a PhD from the University of Toronto and talk about Jacques Maritain and Etienne Gilson. He associated being thoughtful with being earthy. He had an early beard and wore a beret sometimes. He could have gotten away with even weirder hats. A year younger than me, he still told me what to buy at K-Mart for the apartment. "You will need this frying pan. And these, these bombs to kill whatever kind of insects will be in the apartment you will find." He had some knowledge of the lay of the loner land. The place he helped me vet was tiny and cheap. Three hundred and thirty dollars a month, but it had a big bedroom, a small kitchen, a bathroom and a walk-in closet hallway to the bathroom. The bedroom had windows that went practically floor to ceiling, and the walls were painted green. The kitchen had linoleum, a round table, a fridge, a sink and a stove, and there was a tiny window over the sink. The best part was it had a screened-in porch about the size of a desk, with shelves on one side and a rackety screen door. The floor of the porch had that green plastic grass you sometimes would see under the meat in a supermarket trying to look fancy. *This meat is from cows that ate fake grass.* We looked at this porch, with its views of needle oaks and fig trees in an open space shared by the houses on two blocks, and thought, "Writing. Reading. Drinking coffee. Drinking beer." The last thing he did before getting back in his car was help me set off the bug bombs, which we both watched fill up the empty apartment through the window in the kitchen door. Then he left. I don't think I ever saw him again. We sent some letters back and forth, but I can never remember how to spell his last name, so have never been able to reconnect. I think it was pronounced *Ah-key-oh,* but is spelled with some odd combination of *c*'s and *k*'s and *h*'s, and when I try to do Google searches, all I get is kinds of sushi and towns in Finland. Old friend, if you read this, know that I tried.

The house was chunky, made of stones, in a neighborhood of wooden Victorian houses and a few old brick apartment buildings. At the end of the block, there was a Covenanter Presbyterian Church, and across from that, there was a parking lot lined with promiscuously growing rose bushes. There were a ton of them. Small red roses, red rosehips in winter and fall. Only once in my time there did I set foot in the lot. The night before he got the used car working and split town to head back to Oklahoma, my neighbor sat drunk and high there with a guy in a pinstripe suit with no socks, his ankles and wrists crisscrossed with spiderweb tattoos. They called me over and offered me a beer. Last time I saw them. The guy who sold him the car came around a few months later and said the police found the Dodge outside of Tulsa. "Damned fool didn't change the name on the title."

The landlady was named J. J. Sweeney. She was maybe in her fifties or sixties. When you are twenty-three, you can't tell the difference very easily. She had one of those plunging pitch accents. I doubt she was from the City of Greensboro, probably from one of those small towns where the movie theater was by now (1993) turned into an antique consignment market where people could bring their most clunky yard-sale cabinets, and there is good barbecue on paper plates. And at the diner, I will take the baked chicken with the pinto beans, onions on top of those, and some greens. Maybe one 1940s pickup truck at the intersection near the two-town elementary school. Kid from there grows up, goes into marine biology, thinking they will make a movie about him. Goes to Cuba, thinks, "They told me there were old cars here. I don't see them." I would like to say that the first time I met the landlady she was on the roof pounding some new asphalt shingles into a spot where a branch fell through, saying, "Don't need roofers. OR ex-husbands," but that was another time. Maybe I was sitting there puzzling over the "Song of the Wandering Aengus" already. Like most landlords who deal with sensitive college students, she had a bad reputation. She didn't want to see any chin studs or nose-rings or earplugs, and had stopped renting to college students. "I don't always like the transformation," she said. "Graduate students are more together." The alternative kids in Greensboro had a different look than kids, say, down on the Lower East Side of Manhattan, where it was impossible to retreat into a house with a backyard and watch fireflies, adult and aggressive energies always around. These were grungier and also milder types.

The property did not look like it had apartments. It did not even have a common mailbox area or multiple doorbells, but it was divided up into six units. If you came up the front path, there was a big stone porch. There were two larger units you could enter from the porch. Upstairs lived a young engineer named James Hadley. He had gone to Stanford and then Johns Hopkins, and he had gotten his first engineering job in Greensboro. At some point during his time there, he acquired a banjo. He had California habits. Owned a kayak and bicycled a lot. Taught me how to make pasta by dumping the boiled water on top of the spinach, and then tossing tofu into the noodles with a lot of fresh ground pepper. He was clean-living, affable and easily amused. On the bottom floor was a retired Illinois policeman, a towering bald man with grey chest hair. He had moved to North Carolina "after leaving the force" and gone into construction. He had the manners of a northerner, so I don't think he was from Southern Illinois. I always assumed that he had busted many a longhair head with his club, and I could imagine a figure in sunglasses with a round helmet wrapped around his head, holding up a plexiglass shield while rocks rained down on him from a rooftop. He would have been a horrible sight up on horseback. In reality, he was a cop who probably had taken his retirement in his early forties. He usually made an appearance with his big belly out on the porch, and once I saw a skeletal African American prostitute say goodbye to him, or at least she was leaving. It was still the age of AIDS and crack, but I have no idea what people were really doing.

In the driveway, there was a carriage house, two one-floor studios. Old Paul, who was the de facto building superintendent, lived on the ground floor and cooked dinners on his hotplate. He was a lean old man with a lovely, soft, flat Greensboro accent, and he owned a lawnmower. Several times a week, he pulled it across all of the lawns on the block, and did this for free, I was surprised to learn. "I do it for exercise." When he pulled the lawnmower, he did this bare-chested, wearing dress pants. Old Paul and I liked each other very much. Hearing that I was looking for work, he once drove me to a Big Lots to apply for a job, but he had not told me where we were going or why we were going there.

He had a dog that cried like no other dog I had ever heard. He told me she was thirty years old and part coyote. The old man had one eye, as he had been wounded in the Battle of the Bulge. After the war, he moved to Baltimore and worked as a jazz pianist, he told me, and he had a job at the Calvert Whiskey company as a watchman that almost killed him. The whiskey, he told me, they kept in enormous vats, and there was a spigot at the bottom of each vat. Come time for his shift, there were little bowls placed under each tap to catch the dripping whiskey, but he could turn the tap and get himself a nice drink. He liked to take a sip at each bowl, and by 1955, he was a full-time alcoholic. His older brother lived in the upstairs apartment of the carriage house and had just gotten out of the army after doing his thirty years. He said, "You come here to Walker Avenue and dry out. Live simple." So he did that. Never touched a drop again. "I would have stayed in the army, too, if it had not been for me losing my eye." His brother lived on the top floor of the carriage house. He was dying, a thin, stooped man who could barely breathe. He smelled like butter cookies. His belly had swollen up the size of a six-month pregnancy, and he was close to ninety. He spoke in an indecipherable, high-pitched whisper that Paul could understand, the same as he understood his shepherd/collie/coyote-mix dog. His eyes were small and round. Paul once knocked on my door to help guide him down the rickety wooden steps through the alcove on the side of the house that led to the apartment on the side of the house.

His brother was going to the hospital to die. Inadvertently, but perhaps curious on some level, I remember my hand grazed his belly as I helped settle him into the car. It felt like an unripe cantaloupe under his shirt. Paul's dog died somewhere in there, too. I remember he told me with tears in his eyes. "Well, I am sad. But he couldn't do anything without me." We may have had the same conversation twice. You can live a long life on canned soup, unlikely though that may be. Rather prominently displayed on his shelf was a large box of Trojan condoms. He gestured to them. "Unlike some people, I keep these around, but I don't bring prostitutes back here."

To get to the back of the house apartments, you stepped up past the garbage cans onto some wooden steps under a roof connecting the main house with the carriage house. There was a door there, and an apartment with two bedrooms, a living room, and a kitchen. When I moved there, Richard was living in this stony cave. Then there were two outdoor staircases, and also a short step down into the backyard where there was an enormous fig tree that, given the climate, did not need to be wrapped up in the winter. The shorter stairs led to the second floor of the carriage house. Then there was a long one, the wood eaten away so you could not step on some steps leading to my tree house.

After Paul interviewed me in a few ways a few times, the next one in the house I got to know was Richard. Richard was a big guy, over six feet tall, with thick dark red hair and a big mustache the same color. He looked like Rusty Jones. In humid August, he liked to keep his shirt off outside too. He looked strong but fat in an unforced kind of no-weightlifting way. On Friday nights, he put a big black flat looking cowboy hat on, a Stevie Ray Vaughn deal, cowboy boots, a vest, and a sort of flowing white cowboy shirt. He had never been outside of North Carolina, except a few times, to Tennessee. I thought maybe this cowboy outfit business was a definite look around Greensboro—hell, there is a W in C&W music—but even so, ignorant as I was, I appreciated his impulse towards self-invention and artistry.

"Where you going, Richard?"

"I'm going to yokie-yokie."

"What?"

"You know, karaoke."

Another time, when I was up in my tree house, he stuck his head around the corner. "I'm with a lady in there. If another lady comes around, tell her you haven't seen me. She might have a gun." Sure enough, about an hour later there was a woman who looked past fifty standing there.

"Where's Richard?"

"I haven't seen him."

"You tell him I was around." Then she left, angry. Must not have been too angry, because she came around months later, and they laughed and joked, and then she left.

Richard once brought me my mail. I had a letter from my friend Jeff in Israel. "You got a letter from Ireland, David." He couldn't read, as I found out when he had me read some sort of summons. "I can't read, David." He never asked me to read anything else, and I never saw anything in the mailbox. We didn't have utilities except for phones if we wanted them, but he didn't have a phone. He occasionally asked to use my phone so he could make booty calls, calling up three women in a row to ask for a date to go to karaoke—yokie-yokie—and beginning each call by crooning the first few lines of a song. "Cr----aaaa-zzzy. Craaazy for being in love. Who? This is Richard."

"This is Rich-ard."

"This is Rich-aaaard. You remember me."

Once he made me come down and eat some Hamburger Helper. "I made you dinner." Another time it was scrambled eggs with a side of pineapple turnover cake he had made, both with some old eggs with bits of shell in them, which made me go upstairs and suddenly puke as if my stomach had suddenly become infested, sad to say, with elvers. He sure was sweet to make them, though. This did make me sad because he was having a hard time making the rent, which was not much. "No light in that damn place," the landlady said. "I can't charge much. And I get this Richard." She had one of those amused hard faces where meanness and niceness are freely at play.

At one point, the old cop hired him for his crew, but he only lasted a week. "I caught that dumbass smoking pot while making concrete.

89

You have to watch these redneck potheads on a site. Get somebody killed or maimed. Cause a whole lot of stuff to go wrong. And it's not the first time I hired him either. Sure, I want to help the guy."

Richard freely volunteered a slightly different version of the story. "He gave me the job because maybe he thinks I can bring him some girls up there once."

"Oh shit. That was pretty nice of you."

"Yeah. He pays for plenty of girls."

All of these incidents seem mixed up in my mind with the sensibility of the guy who lived around the corner from me, on Carr Street, Jim Clark, or as he was once known, the Reverend James Lester Clark, the editor of *The Greensboro Review,* and the man who convinced me and many other graduate students to come to Greensboro to study with Fred Chappell, Alan Shapiro, Stuart Dischell and others over the years. Jim had moved to Greensboro in the sixties as a minister whose politics had been radicalized, he said, by seeing the dirty work of the Florida prison system. For years he had edited an independent newspaper, and then sort of drifted into creative writing. His precise history was hard to discern because he had the habit of trying out the plots of short stories on unsuspecting graduate students. Among other things, he had convinced me that as a child in Miami, he had been struck by a Cadillac and placed in the lap of no less a figure than pre-Revolutionary Fidel Castro, who, attempting to raise money for the Cuban cause from some of the wealthier Cuban residents of Miami, Florida, was struck with tender mercy and tears by the poor spritely blond youth with skinned knees "who could have been my own little Fidelito." He also told me he had rescued a very short, alcoholic short story writer, known to us both, from a pandemonium he caused by mistaking for real a showroom layout of a bathroom in the middle of the local Sears department store. "Everywhere people were yelling, and walking by with open mouths, and finally I found him with his trousers rolled down around his ankles, just sitting there." Other stories seem more plausible now than they did at the time. He was the only person around who seemed to remember when the Klan shot up a rally in 1979, the day the Iranians took the embassy, and he claimed that when he had gone as a crusading journalist to do a story about some Klan guys who eventually got charged, they teased him by showing him a bullseye with his own photo taped up in the middle of it with a hole in his forehead. As elsewhere, people in Greensboro remembered plenty of things they did not talk about but acted upon and which acted upon them.

Other nights, Jim and I drank George Dickel with generic cola and talked about Walker Percy and Flannery O'Connor, whom he revered, though he rarely spoke of religion, though naturally when he taught American Literature, for which I once served as his teaching assistant, he was very colorful about Puritan writers and could make Jonathan Edwards and Edward Taylor come alive with short, typifying images, effortlessly and unobtrusively flexing his Duke Divinity School theological muscles. The protagonists and settings of Hawthorne stories, which he loved, were not too different from the various characters and places he pointed out on Tate Street and Spring Garden. "Those are the bushes I was sitting in when Electro and I were both crying about our mommies dying, and a cop came along and clubbed me, and all we were doing was crying." Electro was a well-known blues guitarist and street character from the days when Tate Street was known as "the Haight-Ashbury of Greensboro." Or, when a particularly menacing overweight fellow who used to stride and glower around while wearing, of all things, a propeller beanie passed on the opposite side of the street. "I call that guy the buffoon because he wears that hat and once threatened my boy." He was a cashier at the off-campus book store that sold discount text books. Sometimes Eric, an African American homeless man with high cheekbones like an El Greco, would skip by in overalls, or he would stumble by in a trench coat, or he would march by in a tee shirt and then march by again, a man of many intense moods. "You ever talk to Eric, David? He is a really weird religious person, but nice. I said hello to him last week, and he quoted me a kind of long passage from Ezekiel. If you ever can't fall asleep, just read yourself a begat chart." The only time I saw Jim act in a ministerial way was when he married two students whose marriage was doomed and druggie. He donned a broad black hat, black jacket, black pants, and a white shirt so that his wife Danielle said, "He looks just like a cardboard canister of Quaker Oats, only he has that long grey beard." He performed the ceremony in a mournful and tender way, in a field behind a house, as if he already knew the outcome. Sometimes, he walked funny because he would buy used shoes. Once he told me to be careful buying used shoes because he once had a pair that started to smell like cat piss in the middle of a meeting with a dean. On everybody else, he spent freely, with his inexhaustible modesty and humor. And he cooked for any student who walked by, too. "Dave, how do you feel about roast pork and mojo sauce?" I would walk by his house a lot, so much so that I feared I was being a mooch, and so kept away one weekend. The next Monday, I ran into him on the street, and he said, "Where were you? You better come by tomorrow. I'm making spaghetti with Bolognese sauce." Sometimes I would drive to the Food Lion with him in late afternoon, as he knew that was when they put the half-off stickers on the steaks.

For so many of us who passed through or stayed in town, Jim was like a father who could also be our mother. When Fred Chappell won the T. S. Eliot Award, he said, "I owe as much to Jim Clark as to my mother." Naturally, when I got jumped by a gang of guys and blackjacked on the street one winter night, it was about twenty feet from Jim's front porch, across the alley alongside the Primitive Baptist Church. Jim jumped out of the house with an ancient baseball bat the color of tea as the group ran away, called the cops, sat with me and held an icepack to my head at the kitchen table with Danielle, his daughter Josie peering into the kitchen in her footsie pajamas, until four in the morning and then, pronouncing me concussion-free, poured me a drink and set me up with a pillow on the couch, where I fell asleep watching *Dragnet* and commercials for a local mega-flea market that featured an actor in a gigantic flea suit, which made deep sense to me as I was bugging out. I was never able to write poems about Greensboro that I felt lasted, but when Jim died last year, I wrote this, which I include at the risk of sounding like an essay by Alice Walker or Raymond Carver or something:

Jim Clark's Bardo Party with Greensboro People

Of course, wading pools pop up everywhere,
and people feel welcome to bring kids
for a good time and some strange stuff.
The radio on Grievous Angel 105.2, the station
that plays Graham Parson's funeral pyre
and the gears in a Hank Williams limo sputter,
with I think that is Carole King on one station
buzzing and Rosemary Clooney on another,
and Paul Harvey sounds touchy. Jim has a new house,
sort of split-level ranch but the top floor
slightly askew, rakish, modern. The mud room
turns out to be a doorway in a campus building
about to be torn down, McIver. Once we get there,
Jim does what he always did. He shows us the ropes
of this particularly Bardo party, alcove with open-
backed fireplace to warm us both inside and out.
Tenses wobble. There were a lot of parties then,
with Weber kettles, and sometimes
just a grate thrown over a metal can
loaded with old tarry bits of railroad ties
and broken office furniture. In the corridor
a couple of realtors or ladies from a church
stand disapprovingly, sniff a phantom fart.
They don't like anything that stays fire-lit
or the catfish nailed to the telephone poles.
At one round table there are guys arm-wrestling.
Shouts of "not yet" fill the air. Onesie toddlers
in high furry hats fill corners. Piñatas bend open.
When the prayer bells ring, the beer truck guys

set the keg down and take to their prayer mats
while the procession of former students,
the horror and sci-fi nerds, the edgy
tough guys, unforeseen genii, green oysters
in bushels, pass through from one hallway
and some derelicts come from another
and pass in circles. Danielle pours another cup
of coffee because it is ten a.m. and the foxgloves
are full of bees. Jim leans over in his seat, plucks
a garter snake up from down there and tosses
it over his shoulder. "I feel like St. Patrick, Dave."

See what I mean. Terrible. Jim didn't listen to music like that. It's hard to write poetry about such a time and such a place. Maybe the whole retrospective approach to anything is just doomed.

Meanwhile, back on Walker Avenue, it was still my first January there, and I was, as usual, working on some poems, and getting ready to maybe get some beers, when Richard was at the door. Richard still lived downstairs, and Young Paul had not moved in. "Hey, Bubba, me and my new friend have some beer. I found him, and he's going to live here, too."

That was Young Paul.

That night, he wore a brown corduroy jacket and a black cowboy hat. Like knows like. Young Paul was in his forties, clean-shaven and bright-eyed. "We are going to be neighbors." As sometimes happens with people you actually will come to care about, he annoyed me right away. "Where you from? Richard says NEW York or PITTSburgh. I am from OKLAhoma."

"Bubba, we got some beers downstairs," Richard said. But I was going out.

One morning, a few days later, I saw the new Paul standing across the street at a bus stop. The bus came by perhaps twice a day, and he was the only person I ever saw standing there. Walker was not a busy street, but it egressed onto a road that led to an overpass. He did not have his cowboy hat on, but he wore the same jacket and a tie. He was carrying a clipboard. "New job! And I just moved here. Working at a storage facility as a supervisor. We also rent forklifts. Not bad."

The winter fastened down on the city, with ice storms for a week or so. Spring began to arrive in February. Over the course of the winter, I began to hear the fragments of Paul's story, which was awful. Wife run off the road by a truck in the middle of the night in Texas, and she was a good driver. Home lost. Despair. He was a weepy drunk. "She was a good driver." He would come by when I had friends over, increasingly maniacal, sometimes with a black eye or saying, "My back is all tore up from that gravel those guys and then the cop threw me on." But come Monday, he would be back at the bus stop, in his jacket and tie, holding his clipboard, waiting for the bus. As he stood there, the long-haired cat that lived in the house on the corner rubbed against his leg. "This cat is my little friend," he would call to me as I walked out to my job.

Richard was troubled. "Paul is going to jail. He got in a fight with the police up outside the strip club. That's how his back got all tore up. Keep away from him, Bubba. He's trouble. He showed me the piece of paper. He has a court date."

A few hours later, Paul was at my door. "I am surmising that Richard told you about my legal troubles. I just want you to know that, yes, I have a court date, but my lawyer is getting me a continuance, and it is going to be okay."

I had no idea why I was getting these reports. "Okay, Paul." After that our dealings were very proper. He didn't want me to get the wrong idea about him.

"I am not the person you think I am. You know what I mean. The feeling bad and tragic and getting sloppy. You will see when you meet my mother. She will be coming though here next month. She has an RV. Old Paul says she can use the driveway."

I had a job in the academic advising office, and my job was to make sure all the advisors had the academic folders for the students they advised. I also did a lot of Xeroxing and worked the paper-folding machine and changed the toner and ink on the copier. One day, I tweaked my neck somehow, pulling a ream of colored paper down off a shelf with my left hand. I didn't think it was too bad until that night when I tried to shoot pool and every time I pulled the cue back my left hand began to violently spasm in a way that caused me to shoot the cue ball off the table and onto the one next to it at Witherspoon's Pool Hall. It was a holiday weekend coming up, and I hoped to get a second date, the first one entirely ruined, so I went to the infirmary and was given muscle relaxants.

Passing into the alcove, I told the younger Paul of the diagnosis and treatment. "You mind yourself if you go drinking while taking those muscle relaxants." And then when I went out for a beer, he walked with me. All the pear trees—which smell like sweat socks—were out. Springtime in Greensboro is quite florid. He didn't drink but followed me from bar to bar until finally I had to go home and pretend to be going in to shake him. "It's a rough world out there, David. You have to watch out for people." It was a sort of spooky thing to say. After he disappeared, his apartment was vacant for a few weeks. Then another writing student, Victor, moved in. Victor was like me in a lot of ways. His college roommates from New Jersey visited once, and they told me that when he lived with them, they set up a little studio for him in a closet. I had once spent an entire year of college in the Bronx living in a yurt set up in the middle of a three-person dormitory room. My friend Victor tells me he feels bad about a lot of stuff from those years.

Acknowledgments

Most of all, thank you, Sabrina and friends in various cities. Natalie Reitano read these essays at various stages and helped me grow and revise them all. Thank you, also to the poets and writers who read parts of this book and gave me some sustaining feedback in one way or another as I went along—Victor Cruz, Terry Kennedy, Gregory Lawless, Fred Marchant, Robert Pinsky, Tom Yuill, Mike Riello, Stephanie Burt, Daniel Evans Pritchard, Alan Shapiro, Tony Hoagland, Michael Todd Steffen, Tanya Larkin, Jennifer Barber, Sven Birkerts, David Rivard, and Margaret Muirhead. The parts of this book that remember people and dialogue are no doubt distorted by the effects of memory and writing. "Remarks on Walking Around Boston" originally appeared in *The Rumpus*. "Strange Digs and Jim Clark," "Jazz Vocalists, Other Vocalists, Poetry and the Technologies of Voice" and "Katie Peterson's Robert Lowell, Other People's Lowell, and the Existential Addressee" originally appeared in *storySouth*. "Anonymous Raincoats—Later Poetry of Seamus Heaney and Tomaž Šalamun in Translation" first appeared in *Charles River Journal*. "Ode to Mentality, or Poetry Needs Weird Subjectivity" appeared in *The Critical Flame*. And, oh yeah, thank you, MARC VINCENZ.

About the Author

DAVID BLAIR lives and works around Boston. Thomas Lux chose his first book of poetry, *Ascension Days,* for the Del Sol Poetry Prize in 2007. His second book, *Friends with Dogs,* was a Must-Read Selection for the Massachusetts Book Awards, and his third book, *Arsonville,* was published as part of the Green Rose Prize Series by New Issues Poetry & Prose. A graduate of Fordham University and the creative writing program at the University of North Carolina at Greensboro, Blair has taught in the MFA Writing Program at the University of New Hampshire, and in the online masters degree program in creative writing at Southern New Hampshire University. MadHat Press will be publishing his next collection of poetry, *Barbarian Seasons,* in 2019

www.davidblairpoetry.com

CPSIA information can be obtained
at www.ICGtesting.com
Printed in the USA
FFHW020635270319
51271831-56758FF

9 781941 196847